A Gastronomic
Tour of the
Scandinavian Arctic

CONVERSION TABLES

The precise imperial equivalents of metric measurements are often complicated fractions. So, for simplification, we have rounded them up or down to the nearest oz or fl oz. Use either metric or imperial measurements — not a mixture of both.

LIQUID MEASURES

American	British	Continental
1 tbls (=3 tsp)	1 dessertspoon	15 ml
1/8 cup	1 fl oz	25 ml
1/4 cup	2 fl oz	50 ml (5 cl)
3/8 cup	3 fl oz	75 ml
1/2 cup	4 fl oz	1 dl
3/4 cup	6—7 fl oz	1 1/2—2 dl
1 cup (1/2 pint)	8 fl oz	2 1/2 dl
1 1/4 cups	1/2 pint (10 fl oz)	3 dl
1 1/2 cups	12 fl oz	3 1/2 dl
1 3/4 cups	14 fl oz	4 dl
2 cups (1 pint)	16 fl oz	4 1/2 dl
2 1/2 cups	1 pint (20 fl oz)	6 dl
2 pints	a little › 1 1/2 pints	a little ‹ 1 litre

WEIGHTS

Butter:		
1 tbls	1/2 oz	15 gm
1 cup	8 oz	225 gm
Flour:		
2 tbls	1/2 oz	15 gm
1/4 cup	1 oz	30 gm
4 cups	1 lb	450 gm
Castor sugar:		
2 tbls	1 oz	30 gm
1 cup	8 oz	225 gm
2 cups	1 lb	450 gm

OVEN TEMPERATURES

	Fahrenheit	Celsius
Very slow or cool	225	110
	250	130
Slow or cool	275	140
	300	150
Very moderate	325	170
Moderate	350	180
Moderately hot	375	190
	400	200
Hot	425	220
	450	230
Very hot	475	240
	500	250

©Torsten Blomquist, Werner Vögeli & Timbro

Food photographs: Björn Lindberg

Design: Eric Ekman

Translated into English by Barry Judd, Monica Mauris and David Noble

Typesetting: LMB AB, Sweden
Repro: MULTI-SCAN, Denmark
Printing and binding: DRUCKEREI KRAFT-SCHLÖTELS, West Germany   1987

Swedish ISBN 91-7566-137-3
U.S. ISBN 0-930267-13-3

Torsten Blomquist
Werner Vögeli

A Gastronomic Tour of the Scandinavian Arctic

First United States edition 1987
by Bergh Publishing, Inc.
276 Fifth Avenue
Suite 715
New York, N.Y. 10001
(212) 686-8551

ISBN 0-930267-13-3

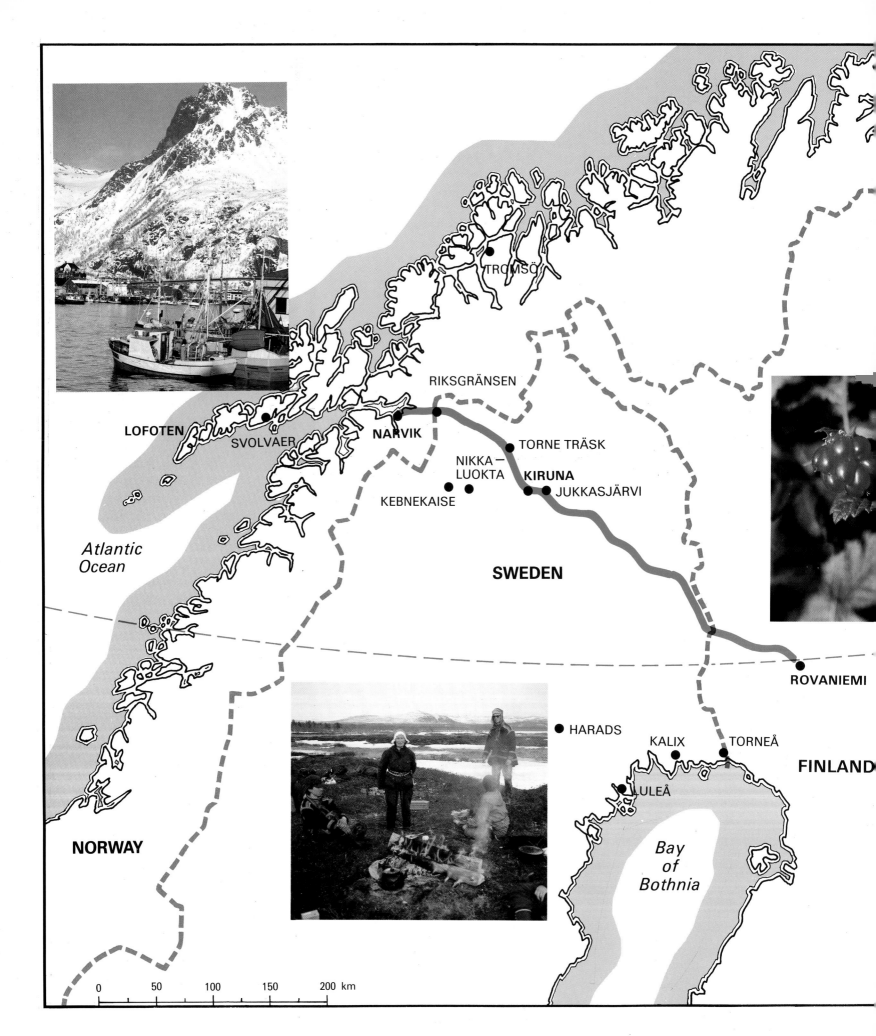

TROMSÖ

RIKSGRÄNSEN

LOFOTEN

NARVIK

SVOLVAER

TORNE TRÄSK

NIKKA—
LUOKTA

KIRUNA

KEBNEKAISE

JUKKASJÄRVI

*Atlantic
Ocean*

SWEDEN

ROVANIEMI

HARADS

KALIX

TORNEÅ

FINLAND

LULEÅ

NORWAY

*Bay
of
Bothnia*

0   50   100   150   200 km

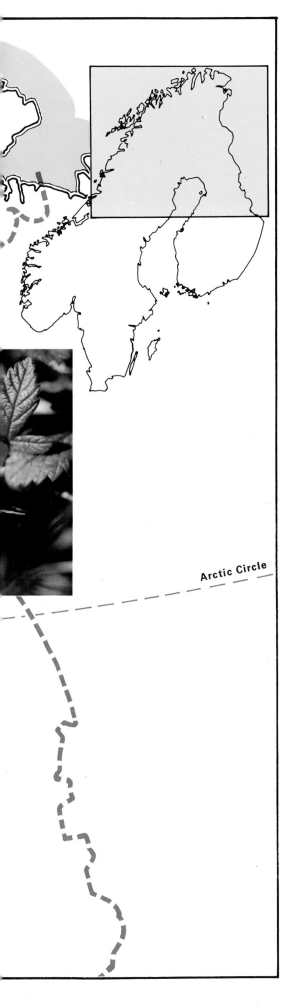

Nature's bountiful larder

Swedish bleak roe caviar, salmon and cloudberry . . .

Daily fare for the inhabitants of the Scandinavian Arctic. For as long as one can recall, people have eaten well in the far north. But without gluttony and excess. Taking only what they need. As natural as nature itself.

In the Scandinavian Arctic, the game and wild berries of the sweeping mountains and rolling valleys, and the marine riches found along the fjord-studded coastlines, have always played a vital role in a landscape not noted for its gentility. For the Laplanders, or Sami as they are more properly called, the reindeer is both a source of income and a means of survival.

The reindeer cook-out is not only the celebration of a successful slaughter; it is a culturally important feast dating back into the mists of time. It is a culinary high-point bearing witness to hard work and superb cooking skills in a difficult climate. The Scandinavian Arctic is a vast region — above the Arctic Circle, an amazing cocktail of jagged coastland, seemingly endless forests, crystal clear lakes and sturdy mountains — lying at the very top of Finland, Norway and Sweden.

Three nations filled with contrasts: Old traditions and modern society cohabitating peacefully. The climate itself is something extraordinary too. The Northern Lights under a sparkling winter night sky....the Midnight Sun, helping the berries to ripen and encouraging animals to grow strong and healthy making a patient people smile....

Werner Vögeli, master chef, and Torsten Blomquist, top Swedish food writer, have taken a uniquely gastronomic journey through the Scandinavian Arctic. And in this book, they have succeeded in capturing the immense riches to be found in the food cultures of the Scandinavian Arctic. The region is one of the kingdoms of nature — and an enormous natural larder.

In the far north, you'll find a wealth of food traditions from surprisingly different communities and regions; the Sami, the fisherfolk, the grouse hunters, and the berry growers.

You'll find different languages being spoken; Swedish, Norwegian, Finnish and Sami, plus a flora of different dialects. Yet Werner Vögeli and Torsten Blomquist have revealed yet another language adding to the mystique: Food! They have simplified, refined, created ... utilizing the fantastic fresh ingredients which have always been found at the Scandinavian Arctic. Culinary skill and recipes of the highest standard tastefully complemented with skilled photography.

This is a unique cook book. For me it is a declaration of love to the north.

Curt Boström
Governor of the Swedish County of Norrbotten

5

Werner Vögeli

Werner Vögeli. By appointment, Chef de Cuisine to his majesty King Carl XVI Gustaf of Sweden. Master Chef to the Royal Court and culinary director of 100 chefs in a restaurant empire with 500 employees.

He is part owner of a group of several globally-renowned Swedish restaurants, Operakällaren, Riche, and Stallmästaregården, based in Stockholm, the capital of Sweden.

Werner Vögeli was born in 1930 in Switzerland. He grew up in Lagnau situated in the famous Emmental cheese district.

Werner Vögeli first arrived in Sweden in 1951. Three years later he became the right hand man of the top chef at the famous Grand Hôtel in Stockholm. In 1955 he was lured to the flagship of Swedish restaurants, Operakällaren in central Stockholm.

At the end of the 1950s and in the early 1960s, while the Operakällaren's outstanding premises were undergoing a major facelift, super chef Werner Vögeli toured Europe further cultivating his skills. He worked in some of the world's leading restaurants in, for example, Bologna, Florence, Milan, Frankfurt and Hamburg.

No other chef in Sweden has served as much food to as many members of the Swedish Royal Family as Werner Vögeli. He prepared food for the late King Gustav VI Adolf and Princess Sibylla. And he has been responsible for the banquets at four Royal Weddings and literally thousands of dinners for Heads of State, both at home in Sweden and abroad.

Nowadays he prepares all the food for the Royal Galas held by Sweden's reigning monarch, King Carl XVI Gustaf and his regent Queen Silvia. Every year, Werner Vögeli prepares the food for the royal couple's private dinner party in honour of the winners of the acclaimed Nobel Prizes.

Werner Vögeli has been honored with innumerable orders and medals, and has received countless diplomas from the world's leading culinary associations.

He is a member of the Club des Chefs des Chefs, the world's most exclusive chef's club.

Werner Vögeli journeyed around the world on his gastronomic travels. With joy, a hearty appetite and never-ending curiosity he enjoys sampling others culinary creations: classical or modern. Nonetheless, Werner Vögeli says he loves Swedish cuisine above all others. And he has a special place in his heart for the fresh basic ingredients.

In the far north of Scandinavia, you'll find the world's finest natural larder, Werner Vögeli proclaims.

Whenever the opportunity arises, Werner Vögeli journeys to the northern reaches of Scandinavia. He loves to walk. To ramble the fells, forests and mountains. To fish for char, talk to the hunters, and inhale the smells and colours of Europe's last true wilderness.

While travelling northernmost Scandinavia, Werner Vögeli makes culinary discoveries in Norway's Lofoten coastal region, marine home to rich quantities of cod, mussels, squid and killer whales.

Or, deep in the wilderness of Lapland, amongst the berries, mushrooms and edible fungi, he gains inspiration for new, startling dishes and recipes.

"I'll never forget," he recalls "the first time I saw the dark meat of grouse. I thought there must be something wrong, something almost too dark . . . Well, now I know better. The grouse has a fine, strong game taste; perfect for an elegant dinner."

The Gold Coast

A raw-cold October morning at the northern tip of the Baltic Sea, the Bay of Bothnia.

Five in the morning.

It's still dark outside.

We're exposing ourselves to the chill in order to catch smallish white fish called bleak, the roe of which gives one of the worlds finest caviar.

We circle around at about two knots.

Towards late morning the dark gradually gives way to a whitish mist. After eight long hours the first catch is winched in.

The nets are chock-a-block, near to bursting point, like an over-filled sack.

Inside the snare is a bustling aquarium of Baltic marine life. Fortunately as the bleak swim in shoals, they will comprise 80—90% of the catch.

In the remainder of the catch one may well find: herring, smelt, lampray, pike, burbot, cod, perch, salmon, ruff and bullhead.

In-fact trawl fishing is a good means of ensuring an ongoing rich abundance of bleak. As the shoal is compressed tightly in the enclosing nets, large quantities of the roe flows into the water allowing nature to take its course....

Along the Bay of Bothnia — nicknamed the Gold Coast — 400—500 people work in the Swedish caviar industry.

About 100 are fishermen working on board 80 to 90 boats. The others, wives, children and grandparents, sit at home in cellars squeezing out the caviar roe from the bleak.

The bleak season bursts into hectic action on the 20th of September every year and ends late October. The weather decides when the fishing slows to a halt. Cold, frost and the first ice herald the season's close.

The catch varies tremendously from one year to the next.

In a super season the hardy fisherfolk bring in up to 80 metric tons. In 1985 around 30 metric tons of Sweden's famed "löjrom" came onto the marketplace via the fisherfolk's own sales and marketing organisation, BD-fisk.

About a third of everything caught is consumed privately.

Between 8—10 percent of the weight of each bleak comprises the caviar. This means that in 1985 roughly 400 metric tons of bleak were caught in all.

Large-scale bleak trawling in order to harvest the caviar got underway seriously in the 1960s. Earlier, such fishing was on a much smaller scale and the techniques used were vastly different.

Only professional fishermen are allowed to pursue their trade inshore, where one is most likely to find the bleak in commercial quantities.

Way offshore, where the chances of finding bleak are highly unlikely, anyone can fish them without having to seek permission.

Fishing for bleak to extract the caviar is extremely profitable. In Sweden one has to pay SEK 500 for a mere kilo! The fishing has become a vital lifebuoy for the last of the professional fishermen in the Bay of Bothnia.

Sadly, the catches in the mid-1980s have shown signs of decreasing. Although prices have rocketed, the indications do not bode well.

"Perhaps we have overfished the area," reflects Kjell Öqvist, chairman of BD-Fisk and a fisherman himself.

"Maybe we should be seeking further afield, but if the truth be known we have no clear idea why our catches are falling."

"Sometimes we find only small bleak being netted. They should be between 12—13 centimeters long. And in good years we've netted whoppers of up to 17 centimeters."

Once landed, the fish are sorted into three different groups — one for the extraction of the roe, one for the fish to be eaten, and the remainder destined to be converted into animal feed.

Extracting the roe is a remarkably skilled craft.

In cellars and garages you will find children and senior citizens alike, sitting intent on carefully squeezing out the valuable roe or caviar. The caviar corns are small eggs filled with a fluid. If squeezed too sharply, the membrane leaks causing the caviar to lose its taste and consistency.

No machinery is used. Only nimble fingers can work sensitively enough to ensure that the caviar eggs are extracted completely undamaged.

Once removed, the undamaged caviar, in Swedish löjrom, is washed, strained and salted. This too is an art form requiring great patience.

"I have tried the löjrom from a number of countries, including Finland, Canada and America," says Werner Vögeli. "But no löjrom can match that found in the Bay of Bothnia; not even löjrom found elsewhere in Sweden. And löjrom from the Kalix' region is something very special. Certainly of world class!"

Werner Vögeli has fond memories of stepping ashore after the long fishing trip.

We were handed bleak poached in lightly salted water. And served with fresh almond potatoes. What a delicacy!

Another arctic delicacy was served us at the home of Elsa Innala in Haparanda, sited smack on the border between Sweden and Finland. It was "dopp i kopp".

DOPP I KOPP

Gutted bleak is lightly poached in salted water with just a smidgeon of white pepper.

Diced raw onion is placed in the bottom of the cup. A little of the water used to poach the fish is poured over the onions — not too much. Serve with melted butter and the poached bleak. You can also serve it with boiled, unpeeled almond potatoes. If the potatoes are peeled, they must be boiled with a slice of lemon, to ensure they retain their fine yellow colour. With the addition of a sprig of dill, the flavour becomes even more delicious. But this refinement is not absolutely necessary.

First, the bleak is rinsed. It is then gutted with the help of a thumb placed in behind the head and twisted so sharply that the gill and intestines fall out. The roe sacs remain; and the roe itself can be pressed out. Afterwards it is rinsed 2—3 times in cold water, while being stirred with a whisk to loosen the membrane.

12

The roe is poured into a container. It has an upper and lower compartment. The upper section boasts holes of about 2 mm in diameter. The roe is rinsed in water. The larger bits, that's the membranes and liver, remain at the top while the actual eggs fall into the second container boasting a finer mesh stopping their further downward journey. The roe is then placed in a bucket to permit excess water to be drained off. The roe is placed in a large container and salted with 45 grammes salt for every kilo of roe. In olden days, when there was no such thing as deep frozen food still more salt was utilised!

As the salt is being stirred into the caviar with a large wooden spoon made of untreated newly cut birch, any excess blood and suchlike is removed. The birch functions like a magnet.

Appetizers

Bleak roe can be used in many ways.
Here are some suggestions for
tasty appetizers.

COLD SCALLOPS WITH
BLEAK ROE
INGREDIENTS:

4 large scallops without coral
10 gm (1/3 oz) butter

PREPARATION:

1.
Halve the scallops across the
grain.

2.
Swiftly "cook" them in the
butter without browning
them, (this takes a very short
time) and allow them to cool.

BLEAK ROE BOUCHEES
(Recipe for puff pastry on page 211)

BLEAK ROE
ON BEEF TARTARE
AND RYE BREAD

BLEAK ROE ON
MUSHROOM CAPS

BLEAK ROE
ON QUAILS EGGS

3.

Place the scallop halves on a wire rack and position a plate underneath. Carefully pour a little of the sauce over the scallops, allowing the excess to drip onto the plate. Refrigerate.

4.

Top with bleak roe and a garnish of chopped chives or red onion.

CHAUD-FROID SAUCE

1 dl (4 fl oz) white wine sauce made with fish stock (recipe on page 210)
1/2 leaf gelatine softened in cold water

Put the softened gelatine in the white wine sauce and bring the mixture to the boil. Allow to cool, using before it sets completely.

CLEAR FISH JELLY

1/2 dl (2 fl oz) good clear fish stock (recipe on page 210)
1/3 leaf gelatine softened in cold water

Put the softened gelatine into the fish stock and bring the mixture to the boil. Allow to cool, using before it sets completely.

This can be used to glaze scallops in the same way as the chaud-froid sauce. It has a very appetizing effect.

BLEAK ROE
IN SMALL
BAKED POTATOES

BLEAK ROE
IN HOLLOW
COOKED BEETS

BLEAK ROE
AND RED ONION
ON CUCUMBER
SEGMENTS

BLEAK ROE
ON ARTICHOKE
HEARTS

COLD SCALLOPS
WITH BLEAK ROE
(Recipe above)

Tiger Beef

Mince finely very lean well
trimmed beef.
Garnish with bleak roe.

per portion:
approx 80 gm (3 oz) beef
30 gm (1 oz) bleak roe

Served with salt and a pepper mill.
Season to taste.

Gulf of Bothnia cocktail

one portion

INGREDIENTS:

200 gm (7 oz) marinated, well drained bleak (recipe on page 33)
4 tbls crème fraiche or thick cream (see NOTE)
2 egg quarters
4 tsp bleak roe
1 small lettuce leaf
1 sprig dill

PREPARATION:

1.
Cut the bleak into small pieces and mix into the crème fraiche.

2.
Put a layer of finely shredded lettuce in the bottom of a small bowl. Place the above mixture on the lettuce, followed by the bleak roe. Garnish with the egg quarters and finely chopped chives.

NOTE: If crème fraiche is not available, a reasonable substitute may be made by lightly acidulating thick or double cream with lemon juice.

MUSTARD SAUCE

1 tbls Swedish or other sweet mustard
1/2 tsp Colman's mustard powder
1 tbls white sugar
pinch salt
small pinch white pepper
1 tsp white wine vinegar
a few drops of water
1 dl (4 fl oz) salad oil

Combine the mustard, mustard powder, sugar, salt, pepper and vinegar in a medium sized bowl. Whisk vigorously and continuously whilst adding the oil in a slow steady stream. Should the sauce separate, add a few drops of water and carry on whisking until it is rectified.

WERNER:
Mustard sauce may be used in the Gulf of Bothnia cocktail instead of crème fraiche, or as a garnish for marinated bleak.

Bleak roe cocktail
with avocado and shrimp
in lemon dressing

one portion

1 avocado
7—10 peeled fresh shrimps
4 tsp bleak roe
lemon dressing

Slice the avocado in half and extract small balls of the flesh with a teaspoon. Moisten the shrimps with the lemon dressing.

Place the avocado balls in the bottom of a small bowl, add the shrimps and bleak roe. Garnish with a sprig of dill and finely chopped red onion.

LEMON DRESSING:

1 tbls lemon juice to 2 tbls
salad oil
salt and freshly ground white
pepper to taste

Fresh artichoke bottom with bleak roe

Bleak roe can be served on a fresh artichoke bottom with crème fraiche and finely chopped red onion.

1 artichoke heart
4 tbls bleak roe
2 tbls crème fraiche

PREPARATION:
Boil the artichoke heart in lightly salted water until it is soft but not disintegrating. Allow to cool. Spread crème fraiche carefully on the artichoke bottom and top it with bleak roe.
Serve on a bed of shredded lettuce with a garnish of finely chopped red onion.

Smoked reindeer open sandwich

On a sparsely buttered slice of coarse white bread, arrange finely sliced **smoked reindeer.** Decorate with a mixture made from one generous tablespoon of **bleak roe,** a little **crème fraiche** and a few drops of **lemon juice.** Garnish with fine slices of **red onion** and **lettuce leaves.**

Baltic Toast and Nordic Toast

Baltic Toast is a composition of **bleak roe, smoked salmon,** and, if you wish, shredded **lettuce** served on a buttery fried crouton, garnished with a **lemon wedge** and a sprig of **dill.**

Nordic Toast is comprised of strips of **marinated salmon,** coated with **mustard sauce** (recipe on page 20) **bleak roe with shrimps** and **chopped chives,** and a **cornet of smoked reindeer with horseradish cream** (whipped cream mixed with grated fresh horseradish to taste), and is served on a rectangular buttery fried crouton, garnished with lettuce and parsley leaves.

29

Skagen Toast

A mixture of **chopped shrimps** and **mayonnaise** is piled neatly onto a freshly fried buttery crouton, and garnished with **bleak roe, chopped chives** and, if you like, **lettuce.**

MAYONNAISE

INGREDIENTS:

1 egg yolk
1 tsp mustard
a pinch of salt
freshly ground white pepper
2 tsp wine vinegar
2 dl (7 fl oz) salad oil

PREPARATION:

1.
Whisk together the egg yolk, mustard, salt and white pepper in a bowl and add half of the oil, little by little.

2.
Add 1 tsp of the vinegar and whisk in the remaining oil, in a slow steady stream.

3.
Finally add the remainder of the vinegar and stir.

WERNER:

This is a neutral mayonnaise, which can be varied, according to personal preference and intended use, by substituting olive oil for salad oil or lemon juice for vinegar. A variety of mustards and other seasoning can be used, for example sweet Swedish mustard, French mustard, cayenne pepper.

PLEASE NOTE: Both the egg yolk and oil should be at room temperature.

Store the mayonnaise in a cool place but NOT in the refrigerator.

Nikkala platter

Marinated bleak, served with boiled potatoes, bleak roe, mustard sauce (recipe on page 20) and crème fraiche or sour cream.

MARINATED BLEAK

INGREDIENTS:

200 gm (7 oz) bleak fillets

PREPARATION:

MARINADE 1:
3 dl (1/2 pint) water
2 tbls white spirit vinegar (12%)
1 tsp salt

Soak the fillets in the above marinade overnight or for at least 12 hours, to remove traces of blood. Discard the marinade.

MARINADE 2:
2 dl (7 fl oz) water
2 tbls white sugar
1 tsp salt
6 crushed white peppercorns
1 dl (4 fl oz) white spirit vinegar (12%)
2 tbls finely chopped chives
1 tbls salad oil

Mix all of the ingredients except the oil and pour over the bleak fillets. Allow to marinate for at least 24 hours and then pour the oil over the fillets. Put into the refrigerator where they will keep for several weeks. The oil makes the fish keep longer and makes the taste milder.

WERNER:

Nikkala is a small village on a peninsula between Haparanda and Torneå. Many of its fishermen take part in the annual bleak fishing.

Bleak roe tartare
from the Gulf of Bothnia

Serves 4—5

INGREDIENTS:

200 gm (7 oz) marinated, drained bleak (recipe on page 32)
4 tbls crème fraiche (or sour cream)
1 hard-boiled egg (yolk and white chopped separately)
4 tsp finely chopped parsley
4 tsp finely chopped pickled beetroot
4 tsp finely chopped onion
4 tsp capers
4 tbls bleak roe
chopped chives

PREPARATION:

Cut the bleak into small pieces and mix with the crème fraiche or sour cream. Shape it as shown and place it in the middle of a plate. Arrange the egg, parsley, beetroot, onion and capers separately around. Place the bleak roe on top of the bleak and garnish with chopped chives.

Fresh asparagus with bleak roe sauce

ASPARAGUS:

Peel the asparagus and boil in lightly salted water. It can sometimes take as little as five minutes, depending on freshness and size. Allow to cool in the water in which they were boiled.

BLEAK ROE SAUCE

INGREDIENTS:

50 gm (1 1/2 oz) bleak roe
1 1/2 dl (6 fl oz) sour cream
1/2 dl (2 fl oz) crème fraiche
the juice of half a lemon
salt and white pepper

PREPARATION:

Mix all the ingredients.

WERNER:
Fresh asparagus is available in Sweden only from the end of April until the middle of June.

Bleak roe
in a puff pastry nest
with creamed parsley
and quails eggs

Serves 4

INGREDIENTS:

120 gm (4 oz) bleak roe
8 quails eggs, hard boiled
100 gm (3 1/2 oz) parsley
leaves without stalks
2 dl (7 fl oz) whipping cream
a pinch of salt
freshly ground white pepper
10 gm (1/3 oz) butter for
frying the parsley
iced water

PUFF PASTRY NEST

300 gm (10 oz) puff pastry
dough (recipe on page 211)
1 egg yolk, beaten

PREPARATION:

1.
Roll out the dough to a
thickness of 3 mm (1/8 inch)
and cut 4 strips, 27 cm (10
inches) long and 1 cm (1/2
inch) wide.

2.
Roll out the remaining dough
to a thickness of 2 mm (1/10
inch) and cut out 4 rounds of
about 10 cm (4 inches) in diameter. Prick with a fork and
brush with beaten egg yolk.

3.
Press one of the strips of
dough around the edge of
each round, and let them rest
in the refrigerator for about
half an hour.

4.
Bake the nests in a 220°C
(425°F) oven for 12—15
minutes until they are golden
brown.

5.
Meanwhile, bring lightly
salted water to the boil and
cook the parsley uncovered
for about 4 minutes.

6.
Strain and refresh the parsley
immediately in the iced water
to retain its bright green
colour.

7.
Squeeze out the water and fry
the parsley for a couple of
minutes in the butter. Add the
cream and boil it down until a
fairly thick consistency is
reached. Season to taste with
salt and pepper.

PRESENTATION:
Divide the parsley between
the four hot puff pastry nests.
Add about 30 gm (1 oz) bleak
roe and decorate with halved
quails eggs and sprigs of flat
leaved parsley.

Savoy cabbage timbale with bleak roe

Serves 4

INGREDIENTS:

100 gm (3 1/2 oz) bleak roe
140 gm (5 oz) savoy cabbage
2 dl (7 fl oz) whipping cream
2 dl (7 fl oz) milk
1 egg
1/2 tsp salt
freshly ground white pepper
butter for the four 2 dl (7 fl oz) moulds

CREAMED SAVOY CABBAGE:

100 gm (3 1/2 oz) savoy cabbage
2 dl (7 fl oz) whipping cream
salt and freshly ground white pepper

PREPARATION:

1.
Bring 3 litres (4 1/2 pints) of lightly salted water to the boil.

2.
Meanwhile, cut out the stem and finely chop or shred the cabbage. Rinse thoroughly in cold water.

3.
Boil the cabbage for about 4 minutes and strain. Retain about 100 gm (3 1/2 oz) for garnishing.

4.
To make the timbale: Place the remaining cabbage in a saucepan. Add cream and milk, season with salt and pepper and boil for about 10 minutes. Mince finely. Stir in an egg. Divide the mixture between the 4 buttered moulds and bake slowly in the oven in a water-bath for 35 minutes at 150°C (300°F). If the timbales are baked at too high a temperature, they will rise quickly and collapse.

5.
Meanwhile, take the cabbage, which was kept aside, and stew it in the cream in a covered pan until done but firm to the bite. Season to taste.

PRESENTATION:

Turn out the timbales onto four warm plates and top each with a spoonful of bleak roe. Surround each one with creamed cabbage and garnish with finely chopped chives.

WERNER:
The components of this dish can easily be made in advance and reheated.

Warm scallop mousse with butter sauce and bleak roe

Serves 4

INGREDIENTS:

FOR THE MOUSSE:

200 gm (7 oz) scallops with coral
3 dl (1/2 pint) whipping cream
1 egg
1 tsp salt
freshly ground white pepper
a pinch of cayenne pepper
10 gm (1/3 oz) butter for buttering four 1 dl (4 fl oz) moulds

FOR THE GARNISH:

200 gm (7 oz) scallops with coral
15 gm (1/2 oz) butter
100 gm (3 1/2 oz) bleak roe

Butter sauce — see basic recipe on page 211.

PREPARATION:

1.
Grind the scallops finely in mixer and then add the egg, salt, white pepper and cayenne pepper. Put the mixture in a bowl and refrigerate until it is completely chilled.

2.
Add the cream, little by little, stirring vigorously with a wooden spoon. When half of the cream has been added, let the mixture rest again for 5 minutes in refrigerator. Then beat in the remaining cream.

3.
Divide the mixture into 4 buttered moulds and bake in the oven in a water-bath for about 35 minutes at 150°C (300°F).

4.
Meanwhile, slice the garnish scallops in half across the grain, keeping the coral in one piece. Season with salt and pepper and fry in 15 gm (1/2 oz) butter in a saucepan (or a sauté pan) for about 2 minutes on each side. The scallops must be handled with great care, otherwise they will become tough and dry.

5.
Cover 4 warm plates with a layer of butter sauce, and turn out the timbales carefully onto them. Garnish with the lightly fried scallops and a green herb, for example dill or parsley.

PRESENTATION:
Serve this dish as an hors-d'oeuvre or main course.

43

Chilled avocado soup
with bleak roe

Serves 5

INGREDIENTS:

2 ripe avocados — about 240 gm
(8—9 oz) pulp
6 dl (1 pint) chicken stock
(basic recipe on page 210)
2 dl (7 fl oz) whipping cream
1 tbls finely chopped chives
salt and freshly ground white
pepper
200 gm (7 oz) bleak roe

PREPARATION:

1.
Cut the avocado in two and
take out the pulp.

2.
Mash the pulp in a mixer
together with the stock. Add
the cream and season with
salt and pepper to taste.

3.
Divide the soup into five soup
bowls and add the bleak roe.
Garnish with chopped chives.

WERNER:
This soup can, of course, be
served without bleak roe but
will be enough for only four
persons. You can also garnish
with slices of avocado.

Jellied reindeer broth with bleak roe

Serves 5

INGREDIENTS:

1 litre (1 1/2 pints) reindeer stock
2 gelatine leaves softened in cold water
bleak roe
chopped chives

PREPARATION:

1.
Mix the softened gelatine leaves with 1 litre (1 1/2 pints) of good clear reindeer stock, bring to the boil and then allow to cool.

2.
Divide the bleak roe into five equal portions and form them into egg shapes in the palm of your hand with the aid of a dessert spoon. Place the egg shapes into soup bowls and put into the freezer for a few minutes to become firm. Then add the cold reindeer broth and refrigerate until it sets.

3.
Sprinkle with chopped chives.

WERNER:
You can substitute any kind of wild game stock for example hare or moose, or even beef or chicken stock.

Chilled cream of cauliflower soup with bleak roe

Serves 5

INGREDIENTS:

1/2 kg (1,1 lb) trimmed cauliflower
1/2 litre (18 fl oz) water
1 tsp salt
2 dl (7 fl oz) chicken stock
(recipe on page 210)
2 dl (7 fl oz) whipping cream
1 tbls finely chopped chives
200 gm (7 oz) bleak roe

PREPARATION:

1.
Trim and rinse the cauliflower and cut it into florets, leaving the tiny green leaves on the stems.

2.
Boil the cauliflower in the salted water for 20 minutes, until it is soft.

3.
Purée it in a mixer with the water, then add the cream and chicken stock.

4.
Taste and add more salt, if necessary.

PRESENTATION:

Divide the soup between five soup bowls. Put 40 gm (slightly less than 1 1/2 oz) bleak roe into each bowl and sprinkle with chopped chives.

This soup may be served hot or chilled. If served without bleak roe, it will only be enough for 4 persons.

WERNER:
If the soup is to be served hot, you can add a little butter, or very small crisply cooked florets of cauliflower.

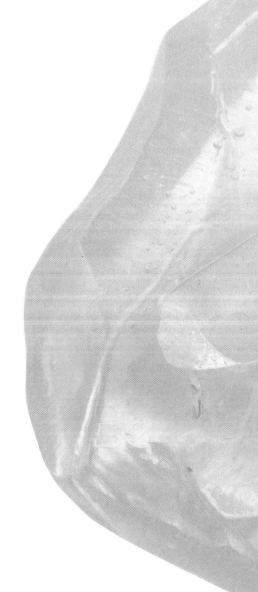

Blinis

15—18 pieces

INGREDIENTS:

2 1/2 dl (8 1/2 fl oz)
buckwheat flour
1 dl (4 fl oz) wheat flour
25 gm (1 oz) yeast
3 dl (10 fl oz) lukewarm milk
1 dl (4 fl oz) sour cream
1 dl (4 fl oz) lager beer
2 egg yolks
2 egg whites
1 tsp salt
clarified butter (for frying)

PREPARATION:

1.
Dissolve the yeast in the lukewarm milk.

2.
Sift the flower and mix all ingredients except the egg whites. Let the mixture rise for a few hours.

3.
Beat the egg whites very hard and mix them into the batter.

4.
Fry the blinis in plenty of clarified butter.

WERNER:
The size of blinis has always been discussed. When the Operakällaren was opened in the autumn of 1961, blinis were made in original Russian pans, about 13 cm in diameter. But the guests found them too large for an hors d'oeuvre. Consequently, we stopped making this size after only a couple of weeks and started making blinis in an iron intended for the very small Swedish pancakes called "plättar", serving two per person. But this did not turn well out either. Some guests were satisfied with one blini, while others wanted two. And by then, the garnish (the bleak roe) was often missing, as the guest had already eaten it with the first blini...

Nowadays, we make the blinis in egg pans, about 9—10 cm (3 1/2 inches) in diameter. Estimate about 1/2 dl (2 fl oz) batter for each blini.

Blinis are excellent to serve with the roe from salmon, bleak, whitefish or trout or, for example, with herring. Serve with sour cream and chopped onions or chives.

Char, salmon trout, grayling, bleak, pike, perch, salmon, and burbot . . .

Make your choice!

Fish in a crystal mountain lake or along the coast. Worm or fly . . . in stream, lake or sea.

In quiet mirror water; or whitecap rapids gushing down from the highland glaciers.

It is your decision.

The water is clear. Clean. Drinkable.

You will find fish aplenty.

Far from the asphalt, stress and dusty roads.

Far and yet so near.

Breathe nature's perfume, the fragrance of the grass, flowers, birch trees, and the reindeer forests. Where the mosquitoes live.

And where smoke from the wood fire dances in the eyes.

In the freedom of the wilds, all you need is a fire and a little salt, and a newly-caught fish, so fresh it's still jumping in the pan.

"One could spend all ones time around a camp fire," says Werner.

At home you can use many ingredients to make a great meal.

But just wait until you try the marvellous fish from the Scandinavian Arctic.

Fish terrine from the Gulf of Bothnia served with bleak roe sauce

Terrine of salmon and pike forcemeat with salmon trout, perch, whitefish and morels, served with bleak roe sauce.

INGREDIENTS:

FOR THE SALMON FORCEMEAT:

800 gm (1 3/4 lb) salmon, skinned and boned
3 eggs
8 dl (1 2/5 pint) whipping cream
1 1/4 tbls salt (about 25 gm)
freshly ground white pepper
a pinch of cayenne pepper
a pinch of grated nutmeg

FOR THE PIKE FORCEMEAT:

300 gm (10 oz) pike, cleaned and boned
1 egg
3 dl (1/2 pint) whipping cream
the marinade from the garnish for the forcemeat
1 1/2 tsp salt (about 10 gm)
freshly ground white pepper

GARNISH FOR THE FORCEMEAT:

100 gm (3 1/2 oz) salmon trout, skinned and boned
100 gm (3 1/2 oz) perch, skinned and boned
100 gm (3 1/2 oz) whitefish or bleak, skinned and boned
5 cl (2 fl oz) dry white wine
the juice of 1/2 lemon
10 gm (1/3 oz) dried morels or a little more than 1/2 liter (18 fl oz) fresh morels
10 gm (1/3 oz) butter
1 tbls finely chopped shallots
1 1/2 tsp salt
freshly ground white pepper
a 2 litre (3 pint) terrine
butter for the mould
kitchen foil

PREPARATION OF THE GARNISH:

1.
Cut the fish into 1 cm (2/5 inch) cubes and marinate them in the wine and the lemon juice for at least a couple of hours (or overnight).

2.
If you are using dried morels, soak them in water. If you are using fresh ones, clean and rinse very carefully. In either case, parboil the morels and DISCARD THE WATER! Cut the morels into pieces of about the same size as the fish.

3.
Sauté the morels with the shallots in butter until all the liquid has evaporated. Allow to cool.

PREPARATION OF THE SALMON FORCEMEAT:

1.
Grind the salmon three times through the finest disc of a meat-grinder or, much easier, grind it in a food processor and chill thoroughly.

2.
Season the forcemeat with salt and pepper and beat in the eggs, one by one, with a wooden spoon. Add the cream and keep on stirring until the farce is smooth.

3.
Make the pike forcemeat in the same way, and also add a little of the fish marinade.

4.
Drain the pieces of marinated fish and the morels and fold carefully into the pike forcemeat.

5.
Butter the mould and line it with the salmon forcemeat. Place the pike forcemeat mixture in the middle and cover with more salmon forcemeat. Smooth down the surface with a knife dipped from time to time in cold water.

6.
Bake in a 200°C (400°F) oven in a water-bath for 1 1/2 hours. After 10 minutes, cover tightly with foil.
The forcemeat will by then be a little stiff and will not stick.

WERNER:
You can, of course, serve the terrine while still warm with a suitable fish sauce.
The different kinds of fish and the morels may also be replaced according to taste, imagination and availability of products.
I use shallots with the morels, because they have a mild taste and, in my opinion, do not spoil the nice aroma of the morels. Ordinary onions are far too dominating.

BLEAK ROE SAUCE:

See recipe on page 36

Salmon
from the rivers of Norrland
— braised in white wine sauce
with dill and bleak roe bouchée

Serves 4

INGREDIENTS:

600 gm (1 1/3 lb) fillet of salmon (skinned and boned) **cut in 4 slices**
1 small leek
1 celery root or stalk
1 small carrot
leek, celery and carrot cut into 3 cm (approx 1 inch) long, thin strips
1 tbls finely chopped shallots
1/2 lemon
2 dl (7 fl oz) fish stock (recipe below)
2 dl (7 fl oz) dry white wine
2 dl (7 fl oz) whipping cream
100 gm (3 1/2 oz) butter
2 tbls coarsely chopped dill
salt and freshly ground white pepper
puff pastry dough (see recipe on page 211)
4 tsp bleak roe

FISH STOCK

salmon head, skin and bones
1/2 onion
the green of a leek, sliced
parsley stalks
1 thyme sprig
a few white peppercorns

Rinse the fishbones thoroughly in cold water, put them in a saucepan. Add just enough water to cover the bones. Add the other ingredients, bring to a boil and let simmer for about 15 minutes.
Skim now and then. Strain the stock, using either a fine strainer or a cloth.

PREPARATION:

1.
Butter a shallow saucepan with about 10 gm (1/3 oz) of butter and sprinkle with the shallots.

2.
Place the salmon slices in the saucepan and season lightly with salt and pepper.

3.
Add the fish stock and the white wine.

4.
Pour the juice of 1/2 lemon over the salmon and cover with buttered paper. Bring to the boil and simmer about 5 minutes.

5.
Put the salmon on a plate and keep warm.

6.
Strain the stock and pour into another saucepan. Add the cream and boil down the liquid to one third, i.e. about 2 dl (7 fl oz). At the last moment, stir in 60 gm (2 oz) butter and add 2 tbls coarsely-chopped dill. If necessary, correct seasoning by adding more salt, pepper or lemon.

7.
Fry the vegetable strips without browning in about 20 gm (2/3 oz) butter and leave them in the butter for about 5 minutes. Salt and pepper. The vegetables should still be crisp.

8.
Place the salmon slices on warm plates, surround with sauce and garnish with the vegetables. Put the bouchée (puff pastry) filled with bleak roe by the side of the salmon.

PUFF PASTRY BOUCHEE

Roll out puff pastry dough into a round, 2 mm (1/10 inch) thick and 3 1/2 cm (1 2/3 inch) in diameter. Make a 4 mm (1/6 inch) broad, thin ring and place it on the round, all along the edge. The inner diameter will then be 2 1/2 cm (1 inch). Bake for 10 minutes in a 210°—220°C (425°F) oven.

If you wish a puff pastry shaped as a fish instead of round, use a cutter in the approximate size of 6×4 cm (2 2/3×1 3/5 inch). Otherwise, the procedure is the same as above.

Salmon mousseline in puff pastry "Queen Silvia"

Serves 4

INGREDIENTS:

SALMON FORCEMEAT:

150 gm (5 oz) salmon, skinned and boned
1 egg white
2 dl (7 fl oz) whipping cream
1 tsp salt
a pinch of cayenne pepper
freshly ground white pepper
20 gm (2/3 oz) chopped truffle
200 gm (7 oz) leaf spinach
a pinch of grated nutmeg
250 gm (9 oz) puff pastry dough

SALMON STOCK

salmon bones
1/2 onion
a few sprigs of parsley
1/2 tsp thyme
a few white peppercorns

FOR BOILING THE SALMON QUENELLES:

1 litre (1 1/2 pints) water
a few sprigs of dill
1 tsp salt

FOR BRUSHING ON THE PASTRY:

1 egg yolk, beaten

SAUCE:

1 dl (4 fl oz) whipping cream
1 dl (4 fl oz) dry white wine
1 dl (4 fl oz) salmon stock
1 tbls finely chopped shallots
100 gm (3 1/2 oz) butter
salt
a few drops of lemon juice
freshly ground white pepper
2 large tomatoes
1/2 small onion
2 tbls coarsely chopped dill

PREPARATION:

1.
Grind the salmon three times through the finest disc of the meat-grinder or mince it in a mixer. Refrigerate the forcemeat for about an hour until it is thoroughly chilled.

2.
Meanwhile, make the salmon stock: rinse the salmon bones in running cold water and place them in a saucepan with just enough cold water to cover them. Bring to the boil and skim. Add the sliced onion, parsley sprigs, thyme and white peppercorns. Simmer for 20 minutes. Strain.

3.
Place a few sprigs of dill in a litre of cold water and bring to the boil. Add the salt and continue boiling for a few minutes so that the water becomes flavoured by the dill.

4.
Take the salmon forcemeat from the refrigerator. Add 1 tsp salt. In order to get the forcemeat firm, it is very important to add the salt immediately. Then add the egg white and stir vigorously, adding the cream gradually. Season with cayenne and white pepper. Stir in the chopped truffle.

5.
Shape the forcemeat with a spoon into four oval balls, approximately the size of hen eggs. Simmer them in the dill-flavoured water for 3 minutes. Remove them with a slotted spoon and allow to cool.

6.
Cook the spinach for a few minutes in lightly salted water. Strain and squeeze out the water. Chop the spinach coarsely and fry in lightly browned butter for a few minutes until the rest of the water is gone. Season with salt, pepper and a pinch of grated nutmeg. Allow to cool.

7.
Take a piece of cardboard and cut two ovals, one 12 cm x 9 cm (4 1/2×3 1/2 inches) and the other 14 cm x 11 cm (5 1/2× 4 1/2 inches).

8.
Roll out the puff pastry dough into 2,5 mm (1/10 inch) thickness. Cut out four ovals of each size, using the cardboard patterns.

9.
On each one of the small ovals, place a bed of spinach and on the spinach a forcemeat ball. Leave 1 cm (slightly less than 1/2 inch) of the edge free all around and brush it with beaten egg yolk. Place the larger oval on top. Press lightly all around the edges to seal.

10.
The original recipe includes an "S" (for Silvia), which is made of a puff pastry strip, 4 cm (1 3/5 inches) long, 4 mm (2/10 inch) wide and 2 mm (1/10 inch) thick. Shape the strip into an S and place it on top of the oval. Brush the top with egg yolk. Place on a baking-sheet and bake in a 250°C (500°F) oven. After 5 minutes, reduce to 200°C (400°F). Bake for another 10 minutes.

11.
Remove the stems from the tomatoes with a small knife. Dip the tomatoes in the boiling, dill-flavoured water and rinse them immediately in cold water. Peel off the skin and cut the tomatoes in two. Squeezse out the seeds. Cut the pulp into small pieces. Fry the chopped onion carefully in butter. Add the tomatoes and cook until all the liquid has evaporated. Rub the mixture through a sieve.

12.
For the sauce, mix in a saucepan: the cream, white wine, salmon stock and chopped shallots. Cook until the liquid is reduced to about 1 1/2 dl (6 fl oz). Strain off the shallots (optional). Take the saucepan off the heat. Add

the butter, little by little, whisking constantly. Add the tomato purée and a few drops of lemon juice. Finally, blend in 2 tbls coarsely chopped dill.

PRESENTATION:
Pour sauce on a plate and place a salmon mousseline on it.

Lightly salted salmon with creamed morels

Serves 6

INGREDIENTS:

1 kg (2,2 lb) fresh fillet of salmon, the middle part
1 dl (4 fl oz) salt
1/2 dl (2 fl oz) white sugar
1 tsp crushed white peppercorns
1 bunch of coarsely chopped dill

PREPARATION OF THE SALMON:

1.
Mix the salt, sugar and crushed white peppercorns. Sprinkle over the salmon on both sides and cover with chopped dill.

2.
Place the salmon in a plastic bag or in a small bowl and cover with plastic film. Leave at room temperature until the salt has melted. Rub each side, making sure the salt and sugar mixture penetrates the fish. Store in refrigerator for 48 hours.

3.
Scrape off superfluous salt and cut the salmon in thin slices. Decorate with a sprig of dill and serve with creamed morels.

CREAMED MORELS

Serves 6

INGREDIENTS:

1 1/2 litres (2 1/4 pints) fresh morels or
30 gm (1 oz) dried morels
15 gm (1/2 oz) butter
2 1/2 dl (8 fl oz) whipping cream
salt and freshly ground white pepper

PREPARATION:

1.
Clean and rinse the morels

2.
Boil the fresh morels for 10 minutes or, if you use dried morels, soak them in water for a couple of hours, then parboil them. In either case, throw away the water after boiling and drain thoroughly. Chop the morels coarsely and fry them in butter until all liquid has evaporated.

3.
Add cream, salt and pepper. Boil down to a thick stew.

Ice fishing on Lake Torne Träsk

A thick layer of wet snow lies atop the ice coating lake Torne Träsk. The sledge sinks almost 10 cm deep into the melting slush.

It is early May, but the ice is still a safe one meter thick.

This far north, the thaw doesn't come until after one's eaten the first midsummer herring in southern Sweden.

The sledge is heavily laden because we are heading into the snow-caped wilderness.

We travel 12 kilometers. One of the runners sticks, but on we continue regardless. The dogs strain on their reins as though everything is a game!

Their tails point skyward. Happy devils. It is the hunting instinct which gets them to pull us so willingly over the lake.

There are 12 dogs on the span: Siberian huskies, Greenlanders and Alaskan malemutes. Prunni (which means "Brown" in Finnish) and Jorm (for "Giant") spring at the head of the pack.

The dogs belong to Svante Inemyr. A bearded mountain fox clad in orange jacket and high leather boots. His dogs mean everything to him. He has more than 20 and someday hopes to make a living raising dogs. But, to raise extra cash, he also works as a security guard at the Björkliden Station. And makes sealskin gloves which he later sells.

Fred Nilsson is a fisherman captaining a boat on Lake Torne Träsk. He lives in Abisko. He shows us how to catch fish under the ice using a net.

We soon catch a red char which really is red, whitefish and burbot.

"Oh no!," exclaims Fred with a mock groan, "not burbot again . . ."

"But burbot is a great delicacy," Werner attempts to explain.

"Not up here, it isn't," says Fred firmly. "Burbot are all bone . . . damn things just make holes in the net."

So that was that. We head in towards land. Light a wood fire on a small mound of stones. We prepare our newly-caught fish directly over the glowing embers. Some we've wrapped in aluminium foil.

"The Sami quality grade the whitefish," explains Yngve Bergqvist who comes from Jukkasjärvi. "The fat and colour tell just how fine the fish is going to taste."

Yngve has brought along some Sami "glödkakor" (a flat, round bread made of flour, salt and water), butter and salt; and we enjoy our meal out in the open air. Despite being on the ice it doesn't feel cold.

Werner cannot stop thinking about burbot. He has some Finnish recipes which he was given by Eila Korkka, who works in the cold kitchen at Operakällaren.

Svante Inemyr lets the dogs rest. He is boring a hole in the ice so that he can fish . . .

Fred Nilsson, Abisko, uses a net to fish on Lake Torne Träsk. But he hates burbot. "Damn things just mess up the net," he insists.

Grilled char and burbot soup

FINNISH BURBOT SOUP

Serves 4 (as a main course)

INGREDIENTS:

8 dl (28 fl oz) water
600 gm (1 1/3 lb) burbot, skinned, filleted and cut into 3 cm (approx 1 inch) pieces
5 large potatoes
1 onion
salt
8 allspice berries
5 white peppercorns
50 gm (1 2/3 oz) butter
1 bay leaf
1 dl (4 fl oz) whipping cream
1/2 dl (2 fl oz) milk

PREPARATION:

1. Peel the potatoes and cut two of them into 1/2 cm (1/5 inch) slices. Cook them in the salted water for 10 minutes.
2. Meanwhile cut the remaining potatoes into large 2 cm (a little less than 1 inch) cubes.
3. Peel the onion, slice thinly, and add, with the potato cubes, to the potato slices which are already cooking.
4. When the cubes are half cooked, add the fish, milk, cream and butter and simmer for 5 minutes.

The intention is that the first two potatoes disintegrate and thicken the soup.

Sprinkle with chopped fresh herbs, or even onion stalks and serve at once.

SALTED BURBOT ROE

650 gm (1 1/2 lb) burbot roe
30 gm (1 oz) salt

1. Wash the roe well, taking care to remove all the membranes and blood.
2. Whisk the roe with the salt.

SERVING SUGGESTIONS:

May be served with blinis, sour cream and chopped onion or on fried buttery toast with sour cream and chopped onion.

Also tastes extremely good mixed with crème fraiche or sour cream, and chopped onions, spread on crispbread.

Foil baked mountain fish with fresh bread. Could one ask for a better meal? The fish is placed directly over the flames. The result is very tasty indeed.

Torsten Blomquist and Werner Vögeli on Lake Torne Träsk — with the famous Lapporten Mountain as a majestic backdrop.

Fried char with sorrel cream

Serves 4

INGREDIENTS:

600 gm (1 1/3 lb) fillets of char
2 dl (7 fl oz) whipping cream
40 gm (1 1/3 oz) butter
flour
salt and freshly ground white pepper
10 small arctic sorrel leaves, shredded

PREPARATION:

1.
Salt, pepper and flour the fillets. Fry them golden brown on both sides in the butter. Add the cream and reduce by 1/3. Sprinkle with shredded sorrel.

2.
Serve with riced or boiled potatoes.

NOTE:

Instead of arctic sorrel you can use other herbs, for example ordinary sorrel, chives, dill, parsley etc.

Instead of char you can use for example whitefish, salmon trout or grayling.

Lofoten.
Two thousand boats fighting
for the best cod.

Bang!

At six o'clock in the morning the starting signal goes off.

It echoes between the surrounding mountain peaks.

An armada of cod fishing boats steer out towards the open sea.

Hundreds of vessels, side by side, full speed ahead. Spray rises high as the bows plummet, crashing down deep into the water and up again.

The battle has started.

The battle for the best fishing sites.

The battle for the kilos.

In the first rank you'll find the smaller boats. They fish with long lines and nets. Those that "juksar".

At ten o'clock the next pack of boats get underway.

The large fishing boats charge out in a broad line to their respective fishing zones.

It is a tough competition. The greater the kilos, the better the income. The boat owners get 54 percent, the crew share the remainder.

In 1986 the fishermen got 6 kronor per kilo for the cod. The price is carefully regulated by the Norwegian government.

In January, the first cod swim in from the Arctic to Lofoten. The cod are ready to mate.

The meat is firm and fine, bursting with caviar. During this period the ancestors of the ancient Norsemen call the cod by a special name — Skrei.

"The Skrei is here!" shrieks the Lofoten Post with banner headlines.

It is the most important headline news of the winter in Norway — a sign that the short cod

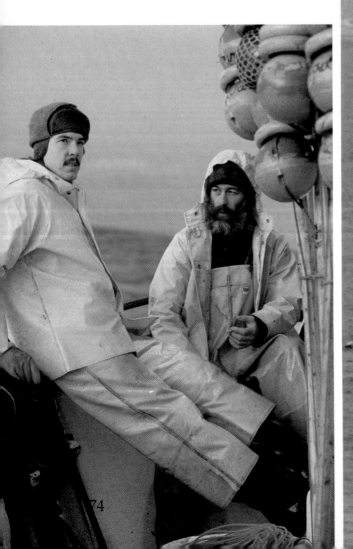

fishing season — lasting only up to 90 days — is under way. By April it's all over.

Lofoten boasts over 100 fish factories.

During the fishing season every tiny village, every single person, young and old, is busily involved in the business of making money from the cod.

Out at sea, they work the nets; on land, it's filleting and salting. The children skip their homework, with their parents willing assent, working down on the quayside gutting cod to earn some extra money.

When the cod season draws to a close in Lofoten, the fishermen head further north to the area called Finnmark (or Lapland). Around 2,000 boats — what a shoal — fish for the Skrei in the Lofoten waters. Some 5,000 fishermen pulling in up to 50,000 metric tons of cod.

Yet the catches were once even larger. In the halcyon 1950s, the fishermen worked around the clock to pull 150,000 tons of cod out of Neptunes clutch.

They've been fishing Skrei at Lofoten for more than 1,000 years. At the end of the last century, more than 30,000 men were employed in the the cod fishing industry.

Some of the fishermen live all year round in Lofoten, a tongue of land with myriad small islands dotted about, pointing out into the Atlantic from northern Norway. Others live a nomadic existence following the cod as it moves along the coastline.

Among them, you'll find Swedes, Icelanders, Danes and Faroe Islanders, all working desperately for the big money that can be made during those few short, intensive months of the Skrei season.

Between January and April, a fisherman can earn anything between NOK 40,000 to NOK 150,000. The size of the catch decides the income.

"It isn't unusual to have an annual salary of over NOK 200,000," says Arne Bardo, a director of the Fiskarnes Bank in Svolvaer.

The fishermen have to fight for their catches in an ever-shifting, turbulent sea. One day the water is still, flat, blue-green, looking like a picture postcard, four to five degrees celsius warm, free of ice thanks to the Gulf Stream, and with the lofty, snow-capped mountains in the background.

The next day the sea can be rough and grim. It's bitingly cold, seasickness threatens and visibility is dreadful.

But the fishermen go out regardless. Even when the weather is stormy.

Only the very worst weather forces the boats back to seek shelter in harbor.

No kilos, no money.

There are five types of fishing carried out in Lofoten waters.

There's Handline: small boats of 25—30 meters length, often handled by just one man who fishes for cod with a long line and hooks. These are the smallest, and most numerous, vessels you'll find in Lofoten's large fishing fleet.

Net fishing: On the net fishing boats, you'll find a three man crew. The net mesh is rather heavy; and the smallest cod ensnared usually weighs several kilos.

Longline: large vessels with 4—5 crewmen which trail long lines bearing hundreds of hooks. One crewman stays on shore fastening shrimp as bait to each hook. As each line is several hundred meters long this can take hours.

Purse seine: the most effective method of fishing which provides the highest quality catch. It is an "on-the-spot" trawl fishing in which the nets are slowly pulled together into the shape of a huge purse. The catch is killed and bled immediately. This ensures top quality meat. Cod weighing up to 40 kilos have been caught in this way.

Trawling: around 75 trawlers travel far out to sea for up to 14 days at a time. They do not participate in the daily cod-fishing race. The trawlers are deep water fish factories. They fillet and salt their own catch on board.

Children remove cods' tongues

Raymond Robertsson is 11 years old. He's cutting out cods' tongues at the quayside in Henningsvaer. He impales the cod's head on a nail and removes the tongue with a sharp twist of a large knife.

Raymond gets 5 kronor a kilo for his craft.

"I'm going to buy a bike with the money," he says with a smile.

Cutting out cods' tongues is an attractive, profitable means of earning some extra cash for the children of Lofoten. It is also a means of learning the skills of the fisherman at an early age. Everyone living in the Lofoten region knows their lives will center around fish and fishing.

Fillets, liver, caviar, tongues, bones . . . everything is collected. And put to good use.

Most of the Lofoten cod is filleted and sold deep-frozen abroad. The tongues are a delicacy which are exported to France, frozen in huge blocks of ice.

A substantial amount of the fish is salted. Selected cod is covered in salt and placed in large piles. After three or four days, the salt melts and courses like a waterfall through the mountain of cod.

The cod is then turned, and salted once again. Afterwards the cod is machine dried.

This means of conserving cod is based on ancient traditions. In earlier days, locals relied upon the sun to dry the cod on special racks sited alongside the fjords.

Even today, large quantities of cod are dried

in the fresh air on special racks or frames. The result is called stockfish. Lofoten's climate is ideal for outdoor drying. The ideal temperature lies between plus five and minus five degrees Celsius. But other key factors affecting quality include sun, rain and insects.

The cod is dried to just 20 percent of its original weight. When moistened later it regains around 60 percent of its weight.

As it loses weight, the price of the fish rockets . . . from six kronor to 60 kronor!

Amongst other places, the dried fish is exported to the Mediterranean — where it is served up as "morue".

Much of the roe goes to Swedish and Norwegian caviar companies. Immediately after the catch the roe is removed. It is rinsed, cleaned and, in centuries-old fashion, sugared and salted; and finally placed in barrels before being sold.

Around 14 kilos of fine salt and seven kilos of sugar per barrel, that is the normal seasoning. But come the end of the season when the roe is more sensitive, slightly larger quantities of salt and sugar are added.

The caviar is placed in special star-shaped containers which ensures that the sugar and salt properly envelopes all the caviar.

After four to five days the barrels are turned and rolled. And after a few more days the barrels are rolled yet again to ensure the salt and sugar seasoning is equally distributed.

Most of the cod livers are boiled. Usually for about 15 minutes at 90 degrees Celsius. The smell is nauseating in the cooking houses, but the cod liver oil produced (600,000 liters from one million liters of liver) is good for children . . . or so it is claimed. Most seem to question that belief when obliged to swallow the mixture!

"The oil is also utilised in the manufacture of perfume, explosives and other oils," says Alf Johansen, a local Henningsvaer tradesman.

From a culinary viewpoint, the cod fishing period at Lofoten is as important as the crayfish or new potato season is in Sweden, for example.

Everyone celebrates with special parties called "møljekalas". Huge feasts are served comprising many local specialities containing cod liver and roe.

"Levermølje" is considered a real delicacy. Visitors will find it served in many fisherfolk homes. With this liver mixture, you'll be presented a home-made pancake-flat bread, which is broken into small pieces and softened by dunking in fish soup. Then liver fat is added, along with sugar or syrup, and the concoction stirred into a white smooth porridge or paste.

"The Lofoten cod is truly amazing, although it needs to be treated with sensitivity," comments Werner Vögeli.

"I prefer to prepare it as lightly as possible so as not to lose any of the natural aroma. It can be grilled, poached, or baked in the oven and served with a good sauce."

"Skreimølje", Lofoten cod with liver sauce, roe and cod's tongue — with beer and fine aquavit — is a true Norwegian classic.

SKREIMØLJE
Cod from Lofoten with cod's liver sauce, roe and tongue

INGREDIENTS:

1 1/4 kg (2 3/4 lb) cod, cleaned, with the head removed
300 gm (10 oz) cods' liver
300 gm (10 oz) cods' roe
8 cods' tongues
30 gm (10 oz) butter and a little flour
2 tbls onion, finely chopped
1 bay leaf
1 tbls white spirit vinegar (12%)
1 lemon
salt and freshly ground black pepper

PREPARATION:

1. Clean and rinse the fish well and cut it into pieces 2—3 cm (1 inch) thick.
2. Wrap the roe in greaseproof paper, cellophane or something similar.
3. Remove the outer skin from the liver. Grip a corner of the membrane with one hand and ease the liver gently out with the other until it is completely free of the skin. Place in a pan with the bay leaf and a little freshly ground black pepper. Put on one side. It is better to squeeze out the liver instead of trying to use a knife, which would only cut through the membranes.
4. Use 2 pans. For the pieces of cod, use a large pan (4 litres = 6 pints) with 3 litres (4 1/2 pints) of water, two tablespoons of salt per litre, the spirit vinegar and 1/2 of the lemon. For the roe, use a smaller pan with less water but the same proportion of salt.
5. The roe needs a little longer cooking time than the fish — 15—20 minutes, according to size. Remove, drain and keep warm.
6. Boil the larger pan of water and let the cod simmer for 6—8 minutes. As soon as the bones can be easily removed the fish is ready.
7. Barely cover the liver with a little of the cod water and bring to the boil Remove from the heat and allow to stand for a few minutes.
8. Place the finely chopped onion in a sauceboat and add the liver sauce mixture. Keep warm.
9. Salt and pepper the tongues, dip them in flour, shake off the excess and fry them quickly in butter.
10. Serve the cod as soon as possible after it is ready. Drain thoroughly, garnish with slices of the roe, the fried tongues and the liver sauce.

Accompany with boiled or riced potatoes. Decorate with the remaining half of the lemon cut into wedges.

A precondition for a 100% perfect cod meal is that the cod, as it is in Lofoten, is absolutely fresh and is poached at the last minute before being served.

Norwegian "Skrei" or cod dries on large triangular racks. The climate in Lofoten is ideal for conserving fish in this manner. The Norwegians eat dried fish which has been soaked in water for four days. The fish is then boiled in lightly salted water. It has a somewhat acidic taste. Should be served with strips of fried bacon, a slice of lemon and a salad.

81

Fricassée of fresh cod from Lofoten in butter sauce

Serves 4

INGREDIENTS:

300—350 gm (10—12 oz) fresh fillet of cod (skinned and boned)
150 gm (5 oz) cod's liver
150 gm (5 oz) cod's roe
4 cods' tongues
salt and freshly ground white pepper
lemon
20 gm (2/3 oz) butter for frying the tongues

PREPARATION:

1.
Wrap the roe in cellophane, gauze or something similar and poach for about 10 minutes in salted water with a few drops of lemon. After 5 minutes, add the liver. Remove both and keep warm.

2.
Cut the fillet of cod into 4 pieces and poach in water with a pinch of salt and a few drops of lemon. Drain and keep warm.

3.
Salt and pepper the tongues and fry them in butter.

Butter sauce — Beurre blanc — see recipe on page 211.

PRESENTATION:

Ladle out a mirror of sauce on a warm plate. Place the fish, roe, liver and tongue on the sauce and garnish with some boiled carrots or other vegetable.

Fresh cod from Lofoten with its own roe, liver and tongue served on a mirror of red wine butter sauce

Serves 4

INGREDIENTS:.

300—350 gm (10—12 oz) fresh fillet of cod (skinned and boned)
150 gm (5 oz) cod's liver
150 gm (5 oz) cod's roe
4 cods' tongues
salt and freshly ground white pepper
lemon
20 gm (2/3 oz) butter for frying the tongues

PREPARATION:

1.
Wrap the roe in cellophane, gauze or something similar and poach for about 10 minutes in salted water with a few drops of lemon. After 5 minutes, add the liver. Remove them and keep warm.

2.
Cut the fillet of cod into 4 pieces and poach in water with a pinch of salt and a few drops of lemon. Drain and keep warm.

3.
Salt and pepper the tongues and fry them in butter.

Red wine butter sauce — Beurre rouge — se recipe on page 211.

PRESENTATION:

Ladle out a mirror of sauce on a plate. Place the fish, roe, liver and tongue on the sauce and garnish with some boiled carrots or other vegetable.

Fried cod from Lofoten with fresh red pepper sauce

Serves 4

INGREDIENTS:

600 gm (1 1/3 lb) fresh fillet of cod (skinned and boned)
15 gm (1/2 oz) butter
1 tbls vegetable oil
salt and freshly ground white pepper

FOR THE PEPPER SAUCE:

200 gm (7 oz) red pepper
2 shallots, about 40 gm (1 1/3 oz)
2 dl (7 fl oz) whipping cream
salt and a pinch of cayenne pepper

PREPARATION OF THE SAUCE:

1.
Cut the pepper in two. Remove the stem and seeds. Rinse and slice the pepper thinly.

2.
Peel the shallots and cut in thin slices.

3.
Put the pepper, shallots and cream in a saucepan and cook covered for about 18 minutes or until the pepper is done.

4.
Pour into a mixer and liquidize. Season with salt and a pinch of cayenne pepper.

PREPARATION OF THE FILLET OF COD:

1.
Cut the fillet of cod into four portions or smaller pieces. Salt and pepper. Fry the fish lightly in a little butter and vegetable oil.

2.
Divide the sauce between four plates and place the fried fillets on the sauce. You can also arrange the fillets in a serving dish and serve the sauce separately.

3.
Serve with rice or boiled potatoes.

WERNER:

According to your own taste and imagination, you may, of course, season the sauce with a few drops of lemon, white wine or crème fraiche etc.

Garnish with some fine slices of green, yellow and red peppers fried in a little olive oil.

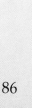

Freshly-fried cods' tongues with seasonal salad

Salt and pepper the cods' tongues and fry them. Let them cool a little and serve them with a salad of the season, as an hors-d'oeuvre or main course.

Marinated fillet of cod with tomato sauce

INGREDIENTS:

1 kg (2,2 lb) fresh fillet of cod, boned but not skinned
1/2 dl (2 fl oz) salt
1/2 dl (2 fl oz) white sugar
10 crushed white peppercorns
5 large sprigs of dill

PREPARATION:

1.
Mix the salt, sugar and crushed white peppercorns.

2.
Rub both sides of the fillet with the mixture. Chop the dill coarsely and sprinkle it over.

3.
Leave the cod at room temperature for about one hour or until the salt and sugar mixture starts melting. Rub the fillet again and refrigerate for about 24 hours, the skin side down. Rub a few times more to make sure the salt and sugar mixture penetrates the fish.

FRESH TOMATO SAUCE WITH CHERVIL

Serves 4

INGREDIENTS:

4 large, mellow tomatoes
1 tbls olive oil
2 tbls chopped shallots
salt and freshly ground white pepper
1 tbls fresh chopped chervil or a pinch of dried chervil

PREPARATION:

1.
Bring 1 litre (1 1/2 pints) of water to the boil in a large saucepan.

2.
Remove the stems and dip the tomatoes quickly in the boiling water. Rinse immediately in cold water. Peel the tomatoes and cut them in halves. Squeeze out the seeds and chop the pulp.

3.
Fry the shallots in oil in a saucepan, without browning. Add the tomato pulp. Season with salt and pepper and simmer for about 5 minutes. Liquidize and allow to cool.

Add more salt and pepper to taste and finish the sauce with chopped, fresh chervil (preferable) or a pinch of dried, crushed chervil.

WERNER:

The chervil may, of course, be replaced by other fresh herbs, for example tarragon.

Naturally, the tomato sauce may be served with many courses other than marinated cod.

You can serve it warm with fried or grilled fish. It is preferable then to use butter instead of oil and add a little fish stock or white wine to improve the taste.

If you do not have a mixer or liquidizer, the tomato pieces may be rubbed through a sieve.

Marinated cod from Lofoten with roe and liver

1.

Thin slices of marinated cod with a sprig of dill (see recipe for marinated cod on page 90).

2.

Salted cod's roe (see recipe on page 94).

3.

Poached cod's liver (poached in salt water with whole allspice, bay leaves and a few drops of white spirit vinegar (12%) — allow the liver to cool in the liquid).

PRESENTATION:

Serve with tomato sauce. (The recipe for tomato sauce is included in that for marinated cod on page 90. Do not use chervil but add a little cream instead.)

Lightly fried marinated cod

Marinated cod, lightly fried, is served with cod's roe sauce, i.e. cod's roe mixed with crème fraiche. Garnish with salted cod's roe.

SALTED COD'S ROE

500 gm (1,1 lb) fresh cod's roe
20 gm (2/3 oz) salt

1.
Clean the roe thoroughly, removing all membranes and blood.

2.
Stir roe and salt together vigorously.

WERNER:

You may also serve salted cod's roe with blinis (see page 50), sour cream and chopped onion. On a crouton fried in butter with sour cream and chopped onion.
Mixed with crème fraiche or sour cream and chopped onion on crispbread.

The magnificent view from Rapadalen towards
Rapaselet. It is August. The water still tumbles
down from Sarek's glaciers. The tongue of land
below towards the right is where the waters from
Upper Rapavagge and Sarvesvagge meet the famed
"Rovdjurstorget" — while to the left is Låddepakte
and, just beyond it, Skårki. You can also see
Piellorieppe and Kåtokjåkkå. Further along in the
valley it is possible to catch a glimpse of Skerfe,
Nammatj ("preachers stool") and Tjakkeli.

Black Grouse

The Black Grouse likes nothing more than perching atop a tree. The male is a blazing, glittering blue-black with a somewhat lyre-shaped tail and white wing bars. The female is large and brown, with a somewhat forked tail. The Black Grouse makes wonderful eating.

The female, called a greyhen, can reach up to 40 centimeters; the cock is around 15 centimeters longer. It boasts a colorful red trim above the eyes.

The Black Grouse can be found throughout the Scandinavian Arctic, although is not a common sight in the very far northern reaches.

Capercaillie

A large bird, the Capercaillie male can grow up to 85 centimeters, while the female is around 60 centimeters. The cock bears a dark, rich plumage and sports impressively large tail feathers. Black-grey with red-brown wing spots, blue green breast. The male has whiskers and red comb below the eyes. The beak is white. The Capercaillie hen is similar to the greyhen, although larger and with a red spot sited on the breast.

The Capercaillie loves the coniferous mountain forests and can often be spotted perched atop a pine tree. The Capercaillie courtship is impressive — a belching throaty sound ends with a joyous happy sound reminding worldy wise listeners of a champagne cork being drawn . . .

The Capercaillie can be found throughout the Scandinavian Arctic except in the very remotest mountain regions.

Hazel Grouse

The Hazel Grouse is a forest hen marked by a relatively long tail. Grey brown with black flecks. A black broken band on the grey coloured tail. Usually to be spotted perching in a tree, the Hazel Grouse is found in the mixed forest and woodlands at the northern tip of the Bay of Bothnia in both Sweden and Finland.

Roast hen capercaillie with blackcurrant sauce

Serves 5—6

INGREDIENTS:

1 hen capercaillie, 1,2—1,5 kg (2—3 lb)
plucked and drawn, (ready to roast)
1 thin slice of pork fat to cover the breast
1 tsp salt
freshly ground white pepper
1 litre (1 1/2 pints) feathered game stock
(see recipe on page 210)
or water
3 dl (1/2 pint) red wine
15 gm (1/2 oz) butter + 1 tbls vegetable oil
for roasting the bird
60 gm (2 oz) butter for the sauce
2 tbls blackcurrants (fresh or frozen and thawed)
2 1/2 dl (8 fl oz) mirepoix
(see recipe on page 210)
1 tbls flour

PREPARATION:

1.
Season the bird with salt and pepper, inside and out, and cover the breast with the pork fat. Tie it with a thin, pre-shrunk string.

2.
Preheat the oven to 250°C (500°F). Put 15 gm (1/2 oz) of butter and 1 tbls vegetable oil in a pot and place it in the oven. When the butter has melted, place the bird in the pot, lying it on one side for 12 minutes and then turning it onto the other side, at the same time, reducing the heat to 200°C (400°F). After a further 12 minutes, turn the bird onto its back. Roast for 35—45 minutes in all.

3.
Take the bird out and let it rest for about 10 minutes.

4.
Cut off the legs and the breast. Wrap the breast in foil and keep it warm.

5.
Chop the carcass into pieces and put back in the pot. Fry with mirepoix for a few minutes. Powder with a tablespoon flour.

6.
Add the red wine and stir, scraping from the bottom so that all flavourings are mixed. Add the game-bird stock, then the legs and simmer until the liquid is reduced to about 3 dl (1/2 pint).

7.
Strain the sauce into a saucepan and bring to the boil. Take it off the heat and finish by stirring in 60 gm (2 oz) butter. Add more salt and pepper to taste.

8.
Cut the breast into thin slices and divide it between the plates, onto which you have already ladled a mirror of sauce. Sprinkle with a few blackcurrants. If you present the bird in a serving dish, pass the sauce separately.

PRESENTATION:
To accompany the roast capercaillie, you can serve vegetables of the season or mushrooms and potato gratin.

INDIVIDUAL POTATO GRATINS

INGREDIENTS:
320 gm (11 oz) small peeled potatoes
slightly more than 1 dl (4 fl oz) whipping cream
10 gm butter for the gratin dishes
freshly ground white pepper
4 small individual gratin dishes, each holding 1 dl (4 fl oz)

PREPARATION:

1.
Cut the potatoes into 2 mm (1/10 inch) slices and put them in layers in the buttered dishes.

2.
Mix salt and pepper with the cream and pour it over the potatoes.

3.
Bake in bain-marie (water-bath) in 220°C (425°F) oven for 35—40 minutes. Let the gratins rest for a few minutes before taking them out of the dishes. (Turn the dishes upside down to get the gratins out.)

Roast female black grouse (greyhen) with cream sauce and frost-bitten cranberries

Serves 4

INGREDIENTS:

1 female black grouse of about 1 kg (2,2 lb)
plucked and drawn, (ready to roast)
1 thin slice of pork fat to cover the breast
1 1/2 dl (6 fl oz) mirepoix
(see recipe on page 210)
1 litre (1 1/2 pints) game-bird stock
(see recipe on page 210)
1 1/2 tbls frost-bitten cranberries (see NOTE)
1 tsp flour
2 dl (7 fl oz) whipping cream
10 gm (1/3 oz) butter and
1 tbls vegetable oil for frying the bird
30 gm (1 oz) butter for finishing the sauce
salt and freshly ground white pepper

PREPARATION:

1.
Season the bird with salt and pepper, inside and out, and cover the breast with the slice of pork fat. Tie it with a thin, pre-shrunk string.

2.
Heat the oven to 250°C (500°F). Put 10 gm (1/3 oz) of butter and 1 tbls vegetable oil in a pot and place it in the oven. When the butter has melted, place the bird in the pot. Lay it on one side and roast for 8 minutes. Then, turn it onto the other side and, at the same time, reduce the heat to 200°C (400°F). After another 8 minutes, turn the bird onto its back. Total roasting time is 25—30 minutes. The bird should be pink inside.

3.
Take the bird out of the pot and let it rest for about 10 minutes.

4.
Cut off the legs and the breast. Wrap the breast in foil and keep it warm.

5.
Chop the carcass into pieces and put back in the pot. Fry with mirepoix for a few minutes and make sure it does not stick, which would spoil the taste of the sauce. Powder with a teaspoon flour.

6.
Add the game-bird stock and stir so that all flavourings are mixed. Place the legs in the stock and simmer until the liquid is reduced to about 2 dl (7 fl oz).

7.
Strain the sauce into a saucepan and bring to the boil. Add the cream and reduce to about 3 dl (1/2 pint). Take the pot off the heat and finish the sauce by stirring in 30 gm (1 oz) butter. Add more salt and pepper to taste.

8.
Slice the breast thinly and divide between the plates, onto which you have already ladled a mirror of sauce. Sprinkle with a few lightly warmed cranberries. If using a serving dish, pass the sauce separately.

PRESENTATION:

To accompany the roast greyhen, serve mushrooms or vegetables of the season.

NOTE:

Frost-bitten cranberries are those that have been picked after the year's first frost — if unavailable, use frozen.

WERNER:
If you do not have game-bird stock for the sauce, I would recommend about 3 dl (1/2 pint) white or red wine, boiled down to half the quantity, then topped up with water until there is about 1 litre (1 1/2 pints) of liquid.

WILD MUSHROOM TIMBALE

Serves 5

INGREDIENTS:

300 gm (10 oz) wild mushrooms, cleaned
(2 1/2 dl (8 fl oz) whipping cream
4 eggs
1 tbls finely chopped shallots
15 gm (1/2 oz) butter

1 tsp salt
freshly ground white pepper
a little butter for the moulds
(5 moulds holding
about 1 dl (4 fl oz) each)

PREPARATION:

1.
Cut the mushrooms in small
pieces and fry them in butter
for a couple of minutes.

2.
Add the cream and bring to a
boil. Salt and pepper.

3.
Liquidize and add the four
eggs. Mix well.

4.
Divide the mixture between
the buttered moulds and bake
in bain-marie (water-bath) for
about 25 minutes in a 200°C
(400°F) oven. For an even
better result, bake for 35
minutes at 150°C (300°F),
which makes the timbales rise
more slowly and prevents
them from sinking too fast.

Grouse

Two types of grouse can be found in the Scandinavian Arctic — willow grouse and ptarmigan. The ptarmigan is the smaller of the two; both varieties change coat several times a year. They can be difficult to tell apart. In winter the ptarmigan is all white.

The ptarmigan lives high in the mountains, mates in the cliff clefts. The willow grouse prefers the arctic prairies with birch scrub heather moors and bogs. The latter is found throughout most of the Far North, while the ptarmigan prefers the western ranges.

In the photograph above, a ptarmigan male is captured changing from his winter attire to a more colourful summer plumage.

The new highway linking the Swedish city of Kiruna and Norway's port of Narvik has opened up the entire border area between the two Nordic nations. Thanks to the broad asphalt road, thousands of tourists, hunters and anglers can enjoy the last great wilderness in Europe. It is no uncommon sight to see reindeer, elk, grouse and foxes standing casually by the roadside. And the mountain back-drop is simply breathtaking!

Breast of snowgrouse with quenelles, gravy and frost-bitten rowanberries

Serves 4

INGREDIENTS:

2 snowgrouse of about 400 gm (14 oz) each,
plucked and drawn, (ready to roast)
2 thin slices of pork fat to cover the breasts
salt and freshly ground white pepper
5 dl (17 fl oz) game-bird stock
(see recipe on page 210)
1 dl (4 fl oz) red wine
about 1 1/2 dl (6 fl oz) mirepoix
(see recipe on page 210)
2 tbls frost-bitten rowanberries (see NOTE)
10 gm (1/3 oz) butter and 1 tbls vegetable oil
for frying the snowgrouse

NOTE: There are two varieties of rowanberries in Sweden, only one of which is edible. Check carefully.

FOR THE QUENELLES:

100 gm (3 1/2 oz) well trimmed snowgrouse (or other fowl)
1 egg white
1 1/2 dl (6 fl oz) whipping cream
a little less than 1 tsp salt
freshly ground white pepper
a little butter for the mould

PREPARATION:

1.
Mince the snowgrouse very finely in mixer or meatgrinder. Add salt, white pepper and egg white. Transfer this forcemeat to a bowl and refrigerate until well chilled.

2.
Add the cream, little by little, stirring vigorously with a wooden spoon. Let the mixture rest again in the refrigerator.

3.
Cover the breasts of the snowgrouse with the pork fat slices and tie them with a thin, pre-shrunk string. Heat the oven to 250°C (500°F). Put 10 gm (1/3 oz) butter and 1 tbls vegetable oil in a pot and place it in the oven. When the butter has melted, place the birds in the pot and lay them first on one side, then on the other, for 6 minutes each side and finally on the back. Roast for about 18 minutes in all.

4.
Take the grouse out and let them rest for about 10 minutes.

5.
Cut off the legs and the breasts. Wrap the breasts in foil and keep them warm.

6.
Cook little dumplings (quenelles) of forcemeat in a buttered dish or saucepan. Shape the quenelles in your palm with a spoon, dipped in hot water. Place the dish in a 250°C (500°F) oven for 10 minutes. There should not be any liquid in the dish, only butter.

7.
Chop the carcass, put back into the pot and fry with mirepoix for a couple of minutes.

8.
Add the red wine, scraping the bottom, so that everything mixes properly. Add the game-bird stock. Put in the legs and boil down the liquid to about 2 dl (7 fl oz).

9.
Strain the gravy into another saucepan.

WERNER:
The braised legs may also be boned and cut into dice or strips and sprinkled over a salad, served as an hors-d'oeuvre. They could also be creamed and served with crêpes or an egg dish. Or, of course, served with the breasts — The meat must be cut in very fine dice or strips.

You can also use the legs for the quenelles.

Clear grouse soup with diced vegetables

Serves 4

INGREDIENTS:

1 grouse, plucked and drawn, (ready to cook)
1 1/2 litres (2 1/4 pints) clear chicken stock
(see recipe on page 210)
a small piece of celery root or stalk
a small piece of carrot
a small piece of the white of a leek
fresh herbs — parsley or chives

PREPARATION:

1.
Rinse the grouse inside and out. Simmer it in the stock for about an hour, but check earlier if it is cooked.

2.
While the grouse is cooking, clean and rinse the vegetables. Cut them in fine dice and cook them lightly in a little stock or water.

3.
Cut the grouse breast in thin strips and the legs in small dice.

4.
Divide the meat, vegetables and bouillon between four individual soup bowls or serve it all in a large soup tureen.

Cream of snowgrouse soup flavoured with morels

Serves 4—5

INGREDIENTS:

1 snowgrouse, plucked and drawn, (ready to cook)
a piece of leek (white only)
about 100 gm (3 1/2 oz)
a piece of celery root or stalk,
about 20 gm (2/3 oz)
1/2 onion, medium-sized
10 gm (1/3 oz) dried morels or
1/2 litre (17 fl oz) fresh morels
1 dl (4 fl oz) whipping cream
2 egg yolks
15 gm (1/2 oz) butter
salt
1 1/2 litres (2 1/4 pints)
chicken stock
(recipe on page 210)

PREPARATION:

1.
Rinse the grouse inside and out. Simmer it in the stock for about an hour, but, to be on the safe side, check earlier to see if it is cooked. If the bouillon seems too mild, add a small "bouquet garni" (i.e. the green of a leek, parsley stalks and a bay leaf). Cook the grouse slowly under cover, otherwise too much liquid will evaporate.

2.
While the grouse is cooking, clean and rinse the vegetables. If you use dried morels, soak them in water for a couple of hours. Throw away the water. If you use fresh ones, boil them for 10 minutes and throw away the water.

3.
Cut the onion, leek and celery in thin slices and chop the morels coarsely.

4.
Fry the onion in butter without browning. Add leek and celery and fry for about 1 minute more. Finally, add the morels and fry lightly.

5.
Remove the grouse from the bouillon and pour bouillon over the fried vegetables. Simmer for 30 minutes. Strain off a little bouillon and keep it on one side. Liquidize the vegetables. Pour the mixture back into the saucepan together with the extra bouillon. Mix and keep warm.

6.
Shortly before serving, beat the egg yolks and cream to a froth and mix it with the soup.

7.
Cut the grouse meat in thin strips and divide it between the warm soup plates or put everything in a large soup bowl. Serve immediately. This soup is very light.

WERNER:
Instead of snowgrouse, you may use for example black grouse or capercaillie, which have been damaged by shotgun pellets and are otherwise impossible to serve.

Mousse of snowgrouse served cold

Serves 4

INGREDIENTS:

1 large snowgrouse, plucked and drawn, (ready to cook)
50 gm (2 oz) chicken liver
1 small shallot, chopped
1 tbls extract of grouse sauce
1 1/2 dl (6 fl oz) whipped cream
1/2 gelatine leaf, softened in cold water
2 tbls Madeira wine
salt and pepper
30 gm (1 oz) butter
1 tbls vegetable oil

PREPARATION:

1.
Season the grouse with salt and pepper and fry it in a pot in the vegetable oil and half of the butter. It should be pink inside.

2.
Remove the grouse and let it cool. Remove the fat from the pot. Add some water and boil down. Skim now and then. Keep the gravy for the sauce extract (see below).

3.
Fry the chicken liver quickly in butter with the shallot, salt and white pepper. The liver should also be pink inside.

4.
Remove the liver and allow to cool. Pour the Madeira wine in the pot and simmer a little. Pour the gravy over the chicken liver. Bone the grouse and use the carcass for the sauce extract (see below).

5.
Pass the grouse meat and liver through the finest disc of the meat-grinder (or mince it finely in some other way). Mix the forcemeat with the sauce extract and the softened gelatine. Stir in the whipped cream and add more salt and pepper to taste.

EXTRACT OF
SNOWGROUSE SAUCE:

INGREDIENTS:

the carcass of the fried grouse
1/2 onion
the green of a leek
1/2 bay leaf
thyme
parsley stalks
1 1/2 dl (6 fl oz) water
fat from the frying of the grouse

PREPARATION:

Brown the carcass in the fat or some fresh butter. Add the onion, leek, bay leaf, thyme and parsley and also brown. Add the gravy and water and let everything boil down to about 1 dl (4 fl oz). Strain and boil down to about 1 tablespoon.

SNOWGROUSE MOUSSE IN ASPIC:

Mix 4 cl (1 1/2 fl oz) clear grouse stock with 1/2 gelatine leaf. Put 1 tbls at the bottom of a 1 dl (4 fl oz) mould. Allow to set. Garnish with truffle and fill with the mousse. Remove the mousse by turning the mould upside down.

PRESENTATION:

Serve the mousse with brioche toast or ordinary white unsweetened bread and a few tender lettuce leaves as garnish. Fresh mushrooms and flat-leaved parsley in lemon dressing are excellent with this dish.

WERNER:
This is a good lunch dish, the garnish of which can be varied according to the season, for example asparagus, artichoke hearts and wild mushrooms. Made with truffle, as on the picture, it is an elegant course for the exclusive dinner party. You will find a simpler variety depicted on page 214 of the index.

Cream of hazel-grouse soup

Serves 4—5

INGREDIENTS:

1 hazel-grouse, plucked and drawn, (ready to cook)
300 gm (10 oz) peeled Jerusalem artichokes
a piece of leek (white only)
about 50 gm (2 oz)
1/2 onion, medium sized
2 dl (7 fl oz) whipping cream
1 1/2 litres (2 1/4 pints) chicken stock
(recipe on page 210)
15 gm (1/2 oz) butter
salt

PREPARATION:

1.
Rinse the hazel-grouse thoroughly, inside and out, and simmer it in the chicken stock for about 1 hour. To be on the safe side, check earlier to see if it is cooked. If the bouillon seems too mild, add a small "bouquet garni" (i.e. the green of a leek, parsley stalks and a bay leaf, see recipe on page 210). Simmer the hazel-grouse slowly covered, otherwise too much liquid will evaporate.

2.
While the hazel-grouse is simmering, peel the Jerusalem artichokes and clean and rinse the other vegetables.

3.
Slice the vegetables thinly. Fry the onion in butter without browning, then the leek and the Jerusalem artichokes. Use a large saucepan, which will hold all the stock.

4.
Remove the hazel-grouse.

5.
Pour the stock, in which the bird has been cooked, over the fried vegetables and simmer for about 30 minutes.

6.
Strain a little of the bouillon into a bowl and put on one side. Liquidize the vegetables and pour back into the saucepan with the bouillon. Add the cream and bring to the boil. If necessary, add more salt.

7.
Cut the hazel-grouse meat in thin strips and divide between the warm soup plates or serve everything in a large soup tureen.

WERNER:

If you want the soup more fluffy, whip half of the cream and stir it into the soup just before serving.

Instead of hazel-grouse, you may use other game-birds with white meat, for example partridge or pheasant.

116

The herd of reindeer moves from its winter pastures to the calving pastures. Not so very long ago, it was not an uncommon sight to see a reindeer pulling a sledge . . . in today's motorised world, the snow scooter is the preferred means of speedy, comfortable travel across the snow-clad landscape. Time marches on even in the Scandinavian Arctic!

A time of expectancy on the moors

An around-the-clock eye is kept on the reindeer herd. The Allas brothers each take turns to watch over the valuable animals. Yet, once in a while, when a damp mist sweeps in, the inevitable happens: A reindeer breaks away from the rest of the herd. However, the would-be escapees are usually found quite quickly with the help of the specially trained reindeer dogs.

A relaxing still has settled across the moors.

A time of waiting.

Per Ola Allas brings up his binoculars. Has a calf been born in the last hour or so?

A cow rises slowly, unsteadily from the ground, stands splay legged, shaking her head somewhat uncertainly. A tremor passes through her; is something about to happen in her body?

No, not yet! The cow lays down on the mossy ground again.

It is early May. We are at Kojärvi. The reindeer have started to calve in the moor pastures.

The Allas family have moved their reindeer from the winter pastures to the east. It took several days hard trekking across the moors to reach the spring pasture.

The reindeer would have preferred to continue further westward, towards Norway, heading still higher.

That is where they would have preferred to give birth to their calves.

But the Allas family have decided to break with tradition. Instead, they have opted to keep the animals in the greater safety of the lowland moors. They have erected a three kilometer long fence made of nylon netting, shaped in a half circle like a fishing trawl.

The reindeer follow their instincts. They want to continue pushing on towards Norway. The thought never occurs to them to turn and try to leave from the reverse, open end of the fence. Nonetheless some do try to escape, and are swiftly rounded up by the specially trained reindeer dogs.

"The climate is much kinder here on the moor, especially for the newly born calves,"

explains Per Ola, one of the ten members of the Allas family. "Plus, the fact that we are able to live so close to the herd means there is not as much danger of a young calf being wounded or killed by a wild animal. In this part of the world we have bears, lynx, wolverine and eagles," he adds warningly.

It is the first time in over two decades that the Sami have followed a reindeer herd so closely during the calving period. They maintain a 24-hour watch over the reindeer. The fence is continually being moved to provide access to fresh grazing.

It is a demanding job. The days are long, the work seemingly endless. The opportunities for sleep are few and far between. It is wet. And cold.

A violet sun can shine all night — or it can be damp and misty with snow or driving rain.

The reindeer set the pace, deciding just how pleasant the night will be. If the reindeer appear content to remain in one place for several days, the Allas consider raising a tent.

When the reindeer have cleared the ground of forage, the herd must be moved. Then it is a night in the open for the Allas family. All they need is a blazing birch fire. It is warming. And dries out the footwear.

The youngest members of the family are packed snugly into the snow-scooter's trailing sledge. Reindeer skins on the bottom, tent skins as a roof.

There is probably no better means of sleeping comfortably in the open, fresh air. But don't they ever fall sick?

"They manage alright, although our kids get colds just like any other," says Marit Anne. "And they occasionally get upset stomachs too."

Marit Anne is a Sami girl from Kautokeino in Norway. She is married with Per Ola and they have three children, Nils Johanas, Sara and Juovna, who is seven.

Both Nils Johanas and Sara have proper Sami boots with turned up toes, and wear the colorful Sami head attire. Juovna has trousers made of reindeer skin just like his father and uncles. He can drive the snow scooter and can already use the lasso with pinprick accuracy at a distance of seven metres.

We are deep in countryside where the roads are unknown.

We arrived by plane and snow-scooter.

"It takes hours to travel anywhere on foot," says Marit Anne.

The decision to live close to the reindeer and keep a careful guard during the calving season has deep economic roots. It is just too costly to let the reindeer take care of themselves in the hard environment of the Lapland moors.

In the worst cases, up to 70 percent of the calves have fallen victim to wild animals.

On the gentler moors fewer calves die.

At the beginning of June, when the calving period is over, we hear the experiment was a success. Just a few calves fell to wild animals.

But the unexpected can happen!

The reindeer had been slowly foraging across the moor, we were told. The Allas family had built a camp on the south side. Then they found a cow horribly mutilated.

BEAR!

A large bear had broken through the nylon fence to get into the midst of the herd. Inside the fence, the reindeer cows moved worriedly about making sure their offspring were safe. The bear had probably just awakened from its winter hibernation and was most likely extremely hungry.

The Allas brothers failed to track down the bear.

"But we'll catch the bloody beast yet!"

The brothers are no strangers to shooting bear. They have hunted bear on the Pessisvare and Vaivantjåkko mountain ranges not far from Talma on Torne Träsk. Talma is the Sami village where the Allas family have their main home.

The Allas calving experiment went so well that other Sami families are considering resorting to the same low-stress model.

After a month behind the nearly invisible nylon fence, the reindeer had become practically tame.

The Allas family branded their calves before they were released into the main herd travelling the summer pastures in the Norwegian mountains.

That saved much time before the autumn slaughter.

Then it was time for a party — and a real reindeer repast.

IN BRIEF

There are some 50,000 Sami in the world. Around 35,000 live in Norway, 10,000 in Sweden and the remainder in Finland and the Soviet Union. 25 percent make a living from reindeer.

A day in the life of a Sami

Per Ola Allas boils reindeer meat in stock. During the winter and spring, the Sami eat reindeer meat practically every day. During the summer they eat a lot of fish. And, naturally, vast quantities of luscious berries . . .

Mealtime. Per Ola and daughter Sara.

Nils Johanas and Sara have fun in the play pen. The trailing sledge is vital in the moors . . . it eases transport of wood and fence poles. And functions as a giant cot. The children sleep soundly within its high sides . . .

Coffee and soft Jukkasjärvi bread-cake in the wild. Marie-Louise, Stig, mother Elle-Karin, Sara, Nils Johanas and Juovna, all members of the Allas family. Marit Anne is just out of the photo. At the back, Olof Henrik Heikka, a young relative from Idivuoma.

Night, but there is no darkness. Stig and mother Elle-Karin build a tepee for us. They erect long birch poles intertwined with supple twigs at the top. Two tent sheets are wrapped around the frame, tightly to ensure no rain would get in, keeping the wind at bay . . . there is no chance of us being frozen by the chill spring snow. At the top there is a smallish circular opening specially shaped to ensure that an adequate up-draught is created to draw out the smoke.

Elle-Karin chops at least 15 large armloads of birch branches. She weaves the supple branches into a carpet to be placed on the floor of the tepee. It is warm and insulating.

Inside, the tepee is highly organised. Just behind the firestone, you'll find the kitchen with every cooking utensil and aid; pans, salt and so on. At the sides of the tepee are the sleeping places. And at the front towards the entrance is where the wood for the fire is kept.

Everything is neat and tidy.

A fire blazes securely in a stable square base of birch logs: pieces of birch bark, twigs and birch logs are all that are necessary, and of course a match. No one need freeze in a Sami tepee.

The reindeer are captured with lassos, slaughtered cleanly and tidily. Meat, intestines and blood — everything is put to good use. Even the horn and skin is later sold.

10,000 reindeer at Rensjön

Rensjön lies just a few kilometers west of Kiruna in Sweden. It is November.

Ten thousand reindeer in a herd radiating out into a dozen coralls of different sizes.

Forty thousand hooves rush confusingly about.

We stand in the midst of them surprised. Imagine the scene. Why don't they rush at us? They always avoid us at the very last instant.

It is 24 degrees Celsius below freezing and when the horns of the reindeer clash, the sound reverberates in the cold, crisp air.

The occasional shot as a reindeer is slaughtered pierces the low rumble of the hooves on the frozen wasteland.

The reindeer are separated according to who owns them, some are to be slaughtered. This time everything is unplanned, but so necessary; a vital gathering. The autumn has been rainy and the result is a thick layer of ice under the deep snow already blanketing the mountain slopes.

The reindeer have difficulty scratching below the surface for lichen.

Disaster looms close. Thousands of reindeer just days away from starving to death. Now they have been moved to better pastures.

Nonetheless, some are put into vehicles to be taken to the slaughter house, others fall to a shot in the forehead just outside the coralls. The reindeer herders must kill for their own household needs.

The animals are cleaved with well-trained, skilful hands, piece by piece. Stomach, intestines, spine, throat, legs . . . everything comes apart.

The slaughtered reindeer lies like a lifeless doll. The meat is frozen solid within minutes. Ready for a new reindeer cook-out.

Slaughter at Vitvattnet

A modern reindeer slaughter at Vitvattnet in Tornedalen. It's September and we are out in the forest. The reindeer are separated at impressive speed.

The Sami throw their lassos. An old, but amazingly efficient method of catching an animal. A line lands elegantly to fasten in the horns of the running beast. A Sami rarely misses.

The slaughter itself is well organised, efficient, with skilled craftsmen. Carcasses are hung in smart rows. The intestines are sorted. The blood is also collected. It is stirred with a thick birch stick so that it doesn't coagulate.

Earlier the blood was kept in out-turned reindeer stomachs. These were hung in trees to dry. Then it was converted into sausages and palt, a local dumpling made of potato, onion and meat.

The number of blood-bags hanging in a tree was a sign of wealth. Every part of a reindeer is edible or useable: head, body, legs. Not so long ago, the Sami made palt using the brain, ate the meat of the sinews around the hooves, and boiled the muzzle. It isn't so common nowadays, although does occur.

But a celebratory feast of all the best bits comes after every slaughter.

The Sami cook-out.

"A reindeer cook-out," says Henrik Sarri, a Sami from Nikkaluokta. "It is the reindeer we feast upon, not Sami!"

The reindeer cook-out

All around the world there are examples of national or regional dishes which elegantly reveal the different living cultures of individual nations.

"Of all the dishes which I have established a relationship with during my culinary travels around the world, not one has made as big an impression upon me as reindeer," says Werner Vögeli. "The reindeer kitchen demonstrates quite clearly the kind of hard life the Sami live."

Yet the recipes collected from households with generally limited resources reveal that the Sami womenfolk have been able to master the resources available to them.

It is the pure simplicity of their dishes which makes for their superb greatness. The only thing that could give a professional chef food for thought is the absolutely impossible economy — true, Kajsa Warg says one should make best use of what one has available, yet in this case it just happens to be a whole reindeer . . .!

"I have experienced four memorable reindeer cook-outs. The first was at Harads, the second at Jukkasjärvi, the third at Nikkaluokta, and the fourth, once again, at Jukkasjärvi.

"Probably the best was the one at Nikkaluokta in the home of Henrik Sarri, which reflected generations of Sami cooking traditions.

"For example, no vegetables were served apart from boiled almond potatoes, and there was no other seasoning than salt either in the actual preparation of the food or on the table.

"If anyone had mentioned that to me beforehand, I would have feared a rather tasteless meal. But I can assure you that we ate a feast that was incredible and very, very tasty," recalls Werner Vögeli.

For traditional reasons the Sami have opted not to use seasoning and limit their use of salt, originally as a way of keeping scurvy at bay.

However, there is one exception. Many Sami and Swedes, Norwegians and Finns living in the wilderness use salt in their coffee. This tradition is due to the fact that melted snow water has a low salt content.

At all of the four cook-outs ice-cream with warm cloudberries was served. Ice-cream has been a popular addition to the modern reindeer feast, which like all else dates back to the family get-togethers once held at the foot of the mountains.

On all four occasions both beer and aquavit accompanied the food as well as warm reindeer stock.

A typical reindeer cook-out comprises four or five basic dishes:

reindeer stock with sliced liver and marrow-bone,
butter and bread,
boiled reindeer hindquarters, tongue and black sausage or palt dumplings, almond potatos, (peas),
warm cloudberries with ice-cream and cream, and coffee-cheese.

REINDEER COOK-OUT
About 10 portions

INGREDIENTS:
4 kg (9 lb) reindeer saddle including the fatty area around the tail
1 kg (2,2 lb) reindeer liver
2 reindeer tongues
20 marrow bones, about 15 cm (6 inches) long

For blood sausage and bread:
8 dl (28 fl oz) reindeer blood, frozen or dried
2 dl (7 fl oz) reindeer bouillon (salted water can be substituted)
2 dl (7 fl oz) fat or fat surrounding intestines
3 dl (1/2 pint) flour
1 dl (4 fl oz) grahams flour
1 tsp salt
1,5—1,6 m (1,6—1,8 yards) reindeer intestines

PREPARATION OF SADDLE, TAIL AND TONGUES:
1. Trim the saddle and divide into two to make it easier to cook and when it is cooked, easier to slice. Trim off the fat at the end of the saddle, that is to say around the base and tip of the tail. Put aside a piece that is between 1/2 and 2 cm (1/5—4/5 inch) thick.
2. Rinse and dry the meat. Place it in a large pot with the tongues and lay the tail fat over. Cover with cold water and add a little salt.
3. Bring to the boil and simmer for about 2 hours or until the meat is tender. As soon as the tongues are ready, remove them, skin them and keep them warm.
4. Skim from time to time to keep the bouillon clear.
5. Meanwhile rinse the liver and poach it separately in salted water for about 20—30 minutes until it is completely cooked, i.e. no blood runs when pierced. Allow the liver to cool and then grate. (Naturally the liver can be prepared in advance.)

PREPARATION OF BLOOD SAUSAGE AND BREAD:
1. Divide the intestines into two. Rinse them very carefully and turn them inside out.
2. Whisk the blood and strain it into the warm reindeer bouillon. Add salt and pepper and whisk again.
3. Still whisking, add the two flours. The mixture should be well blended.
4. Trim and rinse the kidney fat, dice it finely

(about 3 mm = 1/8 inch) and, with a spoon (it would fasten in a whisk), fold it into the mixture.
5. Tie one end of a piece of the intestine and spoon the mixture into it. When half filled, tie the open end together with the already tied end to form a loop. Even out the mixture. Repeat with the other intestine.
6. Simmer the sausages slowly in reindeer bouillon for about 1 hour, pricking them with a needle from time to time to prevent bursting.

MAKE THE REMAINING MIXTURE INTO "PALT BREAD":
Add to the remainder of the sausage mix:
4 dl (14 fl oz) flour
1 dl (4 fl oz) grahams flour
1 dl (4 fl oz) fat
1/2 tsp salt
Mix well and form into small ovals. Poach in reindeer bouillon for about 45 minutes.

MARROW BONES:
Just before the meal is due to begin, drop the marrow bones into boiling salted water for exactly eight minutes. The marrow should not run out of the bones; it should be tender and succulent but not too fat.

The bones should be served immediately whilst still hot on warm plates so that the marrows do not set. Long thin specially made birch sticks, sometimes decorated with woollen tassels in the Sami colours: yellow, red and blue, are used to ease out the marrows which are then mashed with the grated liver.

Hot reindeer bouillon is served in cups throughout the meal. After this starter, hot clean plates are set out and the sliced saddle, tail fat and tongue is served with the degreased bouillon from the pot as a sauce. The tail fat is eaten in thin slices or as "butter" with the meat.

Next comes the hot blood sausage and bread with more of the bouillon if so desired.

Finally freshly picked warmed cloudberries with ice-cream and whipped cream. If fresh berries are not available, frozen can, of course, be used.

The meal is rounded off with coffee and coffee-cheese.

This is how the meal was served at the home of Margareta and Henrik Sarri in Nikkaluokta. Inger Anna Kuhmunen née Sarri prepared the cook-out. She lives in Rensjön some miles outside Kiruna along the new road which runs between Kiruna and Narvik in Norway. Hers is the recipe for the cook-out which we have used.

LAPP "GLÖDKAKA" FROM NIKKALUOKTA
About 20 cakes

1 kg (2,2 lb) sifted rye flour
7 1/2 dl (1 1/3 pint) milk
100 gm (3 1/2 oz) melted margarine
2 tsp baking powder
50 gm (1 2/3 oz) yeast
1 1/2 tsp salt
1 tbls sugar (for the yeast)

PREPARATION:
Dissolve the yeast in the slightly warmed milk, add the sugar and amalgamate the ingredients to form a dough. Let it rise. Knead and stretch it well so that the dough becomes more pliable and does not break so easily when it is folded.

Roll out to a thickness of 3—4 mm (approx 1/8 inch) and cut out rounds of approximately 20 cm (8 inches). Prick all over and bake on a hotplate on top of the cooker. It is difficult to give precise timing — it is a question of experimentation.

The reindeer cook-out in Harads was arranged by John Simonsson and family. John was best known as "Lapp-Simon" and was an important man in the reindeer meat industry. His reindeer charcuturie products were sold all over Sweden. He died in 1984.

The basis of the reindeer cook-out is always the same, but many families create their own versions by the addition of extra ingredients. Mrs. Tora Simonsson, for example, added light beer, grated onion, rye flour and corn flour to the recipe for her blood sausage.

At home the Simonsson family served fried, tent-smoked reindeer (suovas) with fried potatoes before the warm cloudberries.

COFFEE-CHEESE
In Jukkasjärvi the reindeer cook-out was arranged by Yngve Bergqvist and Ulf Blomqvist at Hembygdsgården. The cook was Karin Viipola, now married to Yngve.

With the reindeer bouillon was served soft, thin unleavened bread, called rieska, which is baked on the hearth. The Sami used to bake this kind of bread over the open fire in the tepee. (See also Glödkaka from Nikkaluokta).

We were also served "Jukkasjärvikaka", a type of soft cake which is not baked over an open fire, but in the oven, and served with coffee-cheese.

Coffee-cheese has a long history. It is especially common in the Finnish-speaking areas of the far north. We found it in shops to the east: Torneå, Pello, Rovaniemi.

The coffee-cheese is brought out on for-

The bone marrow is carefully scraped out during the reindeer cook-out.

mal or ceremonial occasions: Christmas, funerals — and reindeer cook-outs.

Coffee-cheese squeaks pleasantly between your teeth when you chew it.

There are many modern recipes and most of them are very easy. This is one method we learned from Yngve Bergqvist: to two litres of milk at blood temperature, add two tablespoons of rennet and allow to stand until it curdles. This takes about half an hour. Bring the mixture back to blood heat again, put it into a colander and press out the whey. Bake the cheese in the oven at 200°C (400°F) until it is golden brown, cut it into small pieces and dip it in the coffee.

There are others, we heard, who add a little cream to the milk.

Rennet can be bought at the chemist.

Of course, coffe-cheese was originally made from reindeer milk, and was hung up to dry in the tepee in a reindeer bladder. When the rennet was added, the cheese was pressed into round moulds made from plaited fir tree roots. In the tent the cheese became yellowish with black flecks, slightly sooty from the smoke of the birchwood fires. But inside the cheese was perfectly white and tasted like skim milk cheese but with a discernable taste of reindeer, quite strong but not as powerful as, for example, goats cheese. The reindeer milk, which is thick, was diluted by a third with water.

REINDEER
☐ In Sweden there are approximately 200.000 reindeer, worth about 70 million Swedish Crowns.
☐ The average yearly consumption of reindeer meat in Sweden is 300 gm (10 oz) per person.
☐ The female reindeer — 60—100 kg (130—220 lb) — is called a "vaja". The male — 75—150 kg (165—330 lb) is called a "sarv". Both have antlers, which fall in December/January, although the females, which have a gestation period of 220 days, sometimes keep them until calving time in may.
☐ Reindeer are grey-brown in summer, but lighter in the winter. Wild reindeer are to be found in the eastern Karelia region of Finland and in the woods of Siberia in the Soviet Union, 5.000—6.000 in Finland, 900.000 in the Soviet Union.
☐ Reindeer graze in the mountains during the summers and spend the winters in the woods. They feed on lichen, grass, shoots, herbs and wild mushrooms.

Jukkasjärvi

Jukkasjärvi has always been an important meeting place for the Sami. The church has been a resting place and meeting point for burials, weddings and christenings. The chapels oldest section dates back to 1607.

Bror Hjorth's colourful paintings above the altar remind of a time when hardship, drinking and annual harvest laid their mark upon Lapland. They also reveal how the priest Lars Levi Laestadius (1800—61) arrived with his awesome sermons of dire punishment awaiting all those who failed to avoid laziness and spiritual decline!

Jukkasjärvi is a living village with much to offer the modern visitor: The tourist can hitch up some dogs behind a sledge and take off into the wilds, or risk a breathtaking raft adventure down the gushing river. For the less action orientated, there is a broad cultural offering the local museums to homesteads or ancient Sami storage houses.

Rovaniemi

Head-waiter Pekka Sannakorpi.

Rovaniemi is the capital city of Finnish Lapland. Over 90 per cent of the city was destroyed at the end of World War Two. The city has, especially under the guidance of Finland's famed architect Alvar Aalto, been built up again. Today it is renowned for its sports facilities and as a tourist city with some 32,000 inhabitants.

Some claim that Santa Claus hails from Rovaniemi. With a view across the Kemi river, and a pleasant stroll through a birch walkway from the city center, lies the Hotel Pohjanhovi and restaurant Vita Renen (White Reindeer). There the visitors will find themselves served a kaleidoscope of several of the Scandinavian Arctic's tastiest offerings.

The recipes come from master chef Gunnar Pistokoski who was given them in turn by another Finn over 25 years ago.

ARCTIC RHAPSODY
2 slices of fresh grilled salmon
1 grouse breast, boiled
1/2 reindeer tongue (boiled, seasoned with only salt and white pepper)
2 noisettes of reindeer, full-grown or young animal (fried)
Divide a large serving dish into four parts with potato purée as shown in the picture.

The grouse was served with game sauce (made with wine) and cherries.
The salmon was served with parsley, dill and lemon.
The reindeer tongue was warmed in the bouillon.
The noisettes were browned and served with sliced mushrooms, fried in butter.

The dish was accompanied by pumpkin, frost-bitten cranberries, tomato, cucumber, parsley and a croustade of creamed morels.

— Out of the ordinary and very good, said Werner. Only the preserved cherries seemed a bit odd in this exotic preparation.

Noisettes of young reindeer with creamy green peppercorn sauce

Serves 4

INGREDIENTS:

600 gm (1 1/3 lbs) boned
saddle of young reindeer, well
trimmed
2 dl (7 fl oz) whipping cream
1 dl (4 fl oz) game stock or red
wine
(game stock — see recipe on
page 210)
30 gm (1 oz) butter
1 tbls flour
salt
green peppercorns

PREPARATION:

1.
Cut the meat into 3 cm (1 1/5
inches) slices and flatten them
out to 2 cm (4/5 inch).

2.
Heat the butter in a frying
pan or a shallow saucepan.
Salt the fillets, dip them in
flour and shake off the excess.

3.
When the butter stops
bubbling and starts getting
brown, add fillets and fry
them for 3—4 minutes on each
side (they should be pink
inside).

4.
Remove them and keep
warm. Fry the green-pepper
for 1/2 minute in the same
frying pan. Add the game
stock or red wine and let it
boil down before adding the
cream. Reduce to a coating
consistency. Finish the sauce
with a little butter, if you like.

Garnish with vegetables of
the season, for
example mush-
rooms, salsify,
carrots, fried
potatoes etc.

WERNER:
Elk, roe deer and
venison are
suitable alterna-
tives to reindeer.

Young reindeer chops with rich game sauce and pink peppercorns

Serves 4

INGREDIENTS:

8 young reindeer chops
flour
2 tbls reindeer blood
1 tbls cognac
10 gm (1/3 oz) melted butter
Mix cognac, butter and blood. This will stop the sauce from clotting.
1 tbls chopped shallots
2 dl (7 fl oz) red wine
6 dl (1 pint) game stock (from reindeer bones — see recipe on page 210)
1 tbls pink peppercorns (see NOTE)
salt
20 gm (2/3 oz) butter for frying the chops
30 gm (1 oz) butter for finishing the sauce

PREPARATION:

1.
Season the chops with salt and flour them.

2.
Sauté in butter in a shallow saucepan for about three minutes on each side. Remove and keep warm.

3.
Fry the shallots in the same pan for about one minute. Add the red wine and game stock and boil down to about 2 dl (7 fl oz).

4.
Strain the stock into another saucepan and stir in the mixture of blood, butter and cognac, little by little, until it has a coating consistency. You may not need all of the mixture. Finish the sauce with a little butter and more salt, if necessary.

PRESENTATION:

Divide the chops between four warm plates. Pour sauce over the chops and sprinkle with whole pink peppercorns.

NOTE:
Pink peppercorns can be obtained bottled in brine, which should be used as stated above, or dehydrated, which should be allowed to soak in hot water before use.

Reindeer tongue with salad of early vegetables

Serve freshly-boiled, salted reindeer tongue, preferably lukewarm, cut lengthwise, with a special vinegar dressing consisting of:

1 egg yolk
1 tsp French mustard (of Dijon type, made with white wine)
1 tbls red wine vinegar
salt and freshly ground white pepper

Mix the above ingredients. Add **1 1/2 dl (6 fl oz) vegetable oil,** drop by drop, beating continuously.

Serve with a salad of early vegetables, for example asparagus, artichoke hearts, tender spinach, radish etc

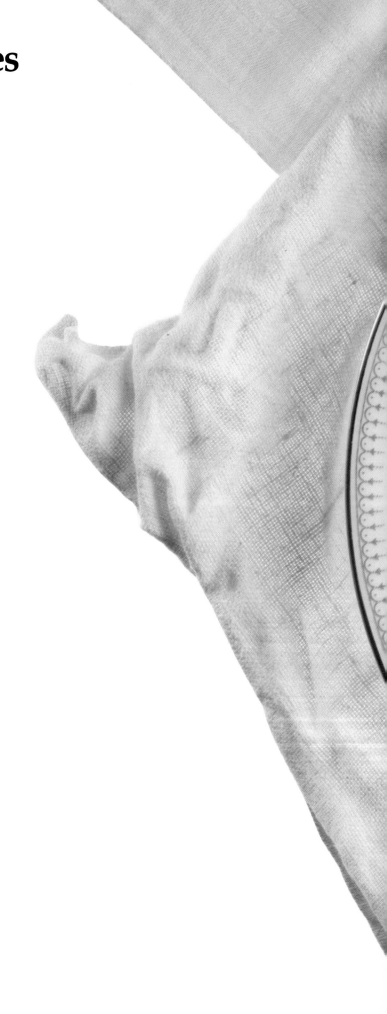

Pâté of reindeer

INGREDIENTS:

800 gm (28 oz) shoulder of reindeer, well trimmed
250 gm (9 oz) fillets of reindeer
400 gm (14 oz) shoulder of pork
400 gm + thin slices of pork fat (for lining the mould)
2 eggs
1 tbls salt
1 tbls flour
freshly ground white pepper
1 tsp thyme
a pinch of grated nutmeg
a pinch of "four spices" (see NOTE)
4 dl (14 fl oz) Madeira
2 tbls cognac

Use a 2 litre mould

MARINADE:

1 dl (4 fl oz) red wine
1/2 medium-sized onion
1/2 carrot
a small piece of leek (white only)
5 juniper berries
1 bay leaf
1 tbls salpetre (25 gm)

PREPARATION:

1.
Trim the shoulder and the fillets, ensuring to remove all sinews and cut the meat in 3 cm (approx 1 inch) dice. Soak for 24 hours in the marinade.

2.
Line the mould with thin slices of pork fat, letting them hang over the edges, enough to fold over and cover the pâté.

3.
Grind the shoulder of reindeer, but *not* the fillets, through a 3 mm disc (1/10 inch).

4.
Grind the shoulder of pork and the pork fat through a 5 mm (1/5 inch) disc. Add the spices and mix with the remaining ingredients.

5.
Put a good half of the forcemeat in the mould. Make a furrow and place the fillets in it. Add the remaining forcemeat. Finally, fold over the slices of lard to cover.

6.
Butter a piece of foil and cover the mould.

7.
Bake in a water-bath in a 200° C (400° F) oven for 2 1/4 hours.

NOTE:
Four spices — a much used mixture, for which each purveyor used to have its own special formula. The ingredients are:
white pepper, powdered cloves, ginger and grated nutmeg.

WERNER:
Instead of reindeer you can use elk, deer, hare or bear.

It can be made richer by adding 1 tbls game extract and 2 tbls chopped truffle. (See picture.)

The flavour can be altered by blending in salted or smoked boiled reindeer tongue, cut in small dice.

Serve the pâté with pickled wild mushrooms or a seasonal salad with freshly fried mushrooms. Sprinkle with lingonberries, fresh or frozen and thawed, to give a colourful and appetizing effect.

Smoked reindeer heart with seasonal salad

Cut smoked reindeer heart in very thin slices and add them to a mixed salad.

For the salad, use for example chicory, curly or rosé, lettuce and strips of carrots and celery.

Sprinkle with a few drops of vinaigrette, mixed in the proportions of 1 tbls white or red wine vinegar to 2 tbls oil. Season with salt and pepper to taste.

WERNER:

The smoked hearts of young elk or deer may also be used.

Game delicacy from Sweden's northern forests

From the forests of Norrland — hazel-grouse and fillet of young reindeer, prepared in two different ways, with garnish of the season.

INGREDIENTS:

2 hazel-grouse (plucked, drawn and larded (i.e. a thin slice of pork fat, covering the whole breast, is tied to it)
200 gm (7 oz) smoked or fresh fillet of reindeer
(boned saddle of young reindeer)
1 litre (1 1/2 pints) fresh morels
(par-boil and throw away the water)
or 40 gm (1 1/2 oz) dried morels (soaked in water)
1 tbls finely chopped shallot or onion
1 tbls fresh lingonberries (or frozen and thawed)
3 dl (1/2 pint) whipping cream
salt and freshly ground pepper
butter and cooking oil
2 thin slices of pork fat

GAME SAUCE:

slightly more than 1/2 kg (1,2 lb) game bones and trimmings
1 tbls cooking oil
1 tbls flour

MIREPOIX:

a small piece of onion
a small piece of celery root or stalk
a small piece of carrot
some parsley stalks
1 bay leaf
4 crushed juniper berries

PREPARATION:

1.
Start with the game stock, which takes the longest time to make. Fry the bones and trimmings in the oil. Just before it is ready, add mirepoix and fry for another minute. Finally, sprinkle with the flour and stir.

2.
Add 1 litre (1 1/2 pints) cold water and bring to the boil, stirring thoroughly, scraping the debris from the pan. Simmer for 1 1/2—2 hours, until the liquid has reduced to 2 dl (7 fl oz). Skim a few times. Strain the sauce into another saucepan.

3.
Meanwhile, roast the hazel-grouse in a 200°C (400°F) oven, in a little oil and butter, first on each side and then on the back for about 15 minutes in all, i.e. 5 minutes on each side and 5 minutes on its back.

4.
Take the birds out and fry the morels. Add the finely chopped shallot (onion) and fry a little more. Finally, add the cream and boil down the sauce to coating consistency.

FILLETS OF REINDEER:

1.
Season the fillets with salt and pepper. Fry them whole in butter, on both sides, for about 10 minutes altogether, depending on the size. They should be lightly fried. Let them rest for a few minutes.

2.
Remove the fillets and pour off the fat. Add the game stock and scrape the debris from the bottom. Boil down to about 1 1/2 dl (6 fl oz). Finish the sauce with about 40 gm (1 1/3 oz) of butter. If necessary, add more salt and pepper.

3.
Cut the fillets diagonally in 1 cm (1/2 inch) thick slices. Ladle game sauce over and sprinkle some lingonberries on top.

4.
Cut slices from the hazel-grouse breasts and place them by the side of the fillets of reindeer. Ladle a little morel sauce over the grouse breast and serve the rest of the sauce separately.

PRESENTATION:

Serve with vegetable purées, for example of celery and carrots.

Saddle of hare in a rich sauce with juniper berries

Serves 4

INGREDIENTS:

2 saddles of hare
10 gm (1/3 oz) butter (for frying the saddles)
1 tbls cooking oil
2 1/2 dl (8 fl oz) game stock (recipe on page 210)
1 tbls whole juniper berries
salt and freshly ground white pepper
1 tsp flour
30 gm (1 oz) butter (for finishing the sauce)

FOR THE MARINADE:

Mix 2 1/2 dl (8 fl oz) red wine with
mirepoix, consisting of:
a small piece of carrot
a small piece of the green of a leek
1/2 medium-sized onion
Cut the carrot, leek and onion in thin slices
1 crushed clove of garlic
parsley stalks
1 bay leaf
4 crushed juniper berries

PREPARATION:

1.
Clean the saddles from sinews and membranes with a sharp, thin knife. Marinate the meat for 24 hours. Keep the trimmings.

2.
Take out the saddles, drain and wipe them with a kitchen cloth or paper towel. Season with salt and pepper and roast them in a 250°C (500°F) oven with the trimmings.

3.
While the saddles are roasting, drain the marinade to dry the mirepoix.

4.
Turn the saddles once and take them out of the oven after about 15 minutes. They should be pink inside. Wrap in foil and keep warm. Sauté the mirepoix in the same frying pan for a minute. Sprinkle with flour and add the marinade. Boil down to half the quantity and add the game stock. Continue simmering until about 2 dl (7 fl oz) of sauce is left.

5.
Strain the sauce and stir in about 30 gm (1 oz) of butter.

PRESENTATION:
Slice the saddles and garnish with vegetables or mushrooms of the season, for example ceps. Vegetable purées made of celery, carrots etc are very suitable.

Sauté the whole juniper berries in a little butter for a couple of minutes and put them in the sauce or sprinkle over the meat.

Fillet of hare with cream sauce and rowanberry jelly

Serves 4

INGREDIENTS:

600 gm (1 1/3 lb) fillet of hare
(boned saddle,
cleaned from sinews)
2 dl (7 fl oz) whipping cream
1 dl (4 fl oz) game stock or red wine
(recipe for game stock on page 210)
30 gm (1 oz) butter
1 tbls flour
salt and freshly ground white pepper

PREPARATION:

1.
Heat the butter in a frying pan or shallow saucepan. Season the fillets with salt and pepper. Dip them in flour, rubbing it in lightly.

2.
When the butter stops bubbling and starts browning, put in the fillets and fry them on all sides for 5—8 minutes altogether, depending on the size. They should be lightly fried, i.e. pink inside.

3.
Remove the fillets and keep them warm.

4.
Pour the game stock into the pan and boil until there is hardly any liquid left. Add the cream and boil down to coating consistency. Finish with a little butter, if necessary.

5.
Cut the fillets diagonally into thin slices. Divide them between four plates and ladle the sauce over. Garnish with vegetable noodles, rowanberry jelly (recipe on page 212) and potato croquettes (recipe on page 211).

VEGETABLE NOODLES:

Cut celeriac, leek and carrots into 1 mm thin slices lengthwise and then into 5 mm wide strips. Boil each kind of vegetable separately in lightly salted water and sauté in a little butter.

Bear

The largest wild animal to be found in the Scandinavian Arctic. The male bear can weigh up to 350 kilos. Heavy legs, thick neck and five claws to each foot. The bear gives birth to very small cubs weighing just 2—3 hectos at birth. Lives in the mountains and the highest, remotest forest regions. Travels over large areas. The male bear can move within an area encompassing around 2,000 square kilometers.

It is estimated that there are around 1,000 bears living in the Scandinavian Arctic. Several hundred are shot every year.

The bear hibernates 5—6 months annually.

Elk

The largest deer in Europe!

Measures up to three meters from nose to tail. A male can weigh over 500 kilos.

The further north you travel, the harsher the climate; and the elk get bigger and ever more noble. They migrate, often in large herds, at high summer southwards towards the lower pastures, or in winter into the forests. There are around 500,000 elk in Sweden. Every year several hundred thousand are shot. Little meat comes onto the open market, however. Most ends up in the freezers of the hunters.

Roast fillet of elk in game sauce with juniper berries

Serves 4

INGREDIENTS:

600 gm (1 1/3 lb) fillet of elk
(Am. moose)
120 gm (4 oz) butter
1 tbls juniper berries
1 tbls finely chopped shallots
1 dl (4 fl oz) Geneva
2 dl (7 fl oz) red wine
3 dl (1/2 pint) game stock
(recipe on page 210)
salt and freshly ground white pepper

PREPARATION:

1.
Heat 30 gm (1 oz) of butter in a low saucepan or frying pan.

2.
Trim the fillet well and season it with salt and pepper.

3.
When the butter starts browning, put the fillet into the pan and place it in an oven at 250°C (500°F). Roast it for about 20 minutes, turning and basting now and then. The frying time depends on the size of the fillet and how you want it done.

4.
Take the fillet out of the oven. Remove it from the pan and keep it warm. Let it rest for about 10 minutes.

5.
Put chopped shallots and crushed juniper berries in the sauce pan. Sauté for a minute. Add Geneva and red wine and bring to a boil. Scrape from the bottom, mixing all ingredients thoroughly. Add the game stock and boil everything down to about 2 dl (7 fl oz).

6.
Strain the sauce and stir in the rest of the butter. If necessary, season with more salt and white pepper.

7.
Cut the fillet diagonally into thin slices. Divide the sauce between four plates and place the meat on the sauce.

PRESENTATION:

Garnish with seasonal mushrooms and vegetables. Serve with potato croquettes (recipe on page 211).

WERNER:
The fillet may also be cut into 2—3 cm (about 1 inch) thick slices and fried in a pan on top of the stove.

September in Börjelslandet just to the north of Luleå. Lily and Erik Holmström and Astrid Sjöberg from Smedsbyn are gathering almond potatos. It is an Arctic delicacy: a small, half-moon shaped, sweet tasting potato. A clear yellow colour inside.

Mushrooms

An amazing range of stunning, delectable and highly edible mushrooms are to be found throughout the Arctic — morel, cep (Karl-Johan), and many, many more with such enticing local names as apelsinsoppar (orange birch boletus), sandsoppar, skogsriskor, skäggriskor; and, of course, chanterelles galore.

Mushrooms are scrumptious "extras" and they comprise an important part of the wilderness pantry found in the far north. The vast majority of mushrooms are ripe and ready for picking during the months of August and September.

Morels arrive somewhat earlier. In May or June. The best are picked when the birch leaves begin to break out. They are found sheltering among the tall pine; or in areas where trees have recently been cut, tracts once swept by forest fire, or where the ground has been trampled. The cap is usually chocolate brown or even a little lighter. Morels are a great delicacy, but poisonous when eaten unprepared. Parboil before use!

In Finland mushroom picking is mostly found in the northernmost reaches. In eastern Finland — especially close to the border with Russia — you'll find myriads of pickers ploughing their way through the mushroom-rich forests in early autumn. Everyone participates. And it is profitable too.

Attractively and devotedly cleaned, sliced into smaller pieces, the mushrooms are delivered in small home-made baskets to the buyers.

The professional buyers conserve, freeze, dry and generally prepare the mushrooms for further distribution. And they ensure that only the best, most tasty mushrooms are passed on to an eager public.

Below is an old Finnish recipe:

PRESERVED MUSHROOMS
1/2 kg mixed wild mushrooms, wiped

Ingredients for the preserving liquid:
6 dl (1 pint) water
1/2 dl (2 fl oz) oil for frying
1/2 medium sized onion, chopped
1 clove of garlic, finely chopped
1 dl (4 fl oz) vinegar
1/2 dl (2 fl oz) white spirit vinegar (12%)
1/2 dl (2 fl oz) white sugar
1 tbls salt
5 white peppercorns
1 bay leaf
1 pinch fennel seeds plus 2 stalks
1 pinch ground coriander
1 pinch dried thyme
parsley stalks

PREPARATION:

1. Carefully wash and dry a jar of a suitable size and place the mushrooms in it as tightly as possible without crushing them.
2. Sweat the onions in the oil until they are transparent. Do not allow them to colour.
3. Add the remaining ingredients to the onions and boil for five minutes.
4. Strain the boiling liquid over the mushrooms, making sure that they are completely covered.
5. Allow to cool and then seal the jar.

The day's picking is over; the baskets are delivered to the professional buyers. Taavi Niskanen's small factory in Pyhäjoki also manufactures lingonberry liqueur.

Cheese from Västerbotten baked in puff pastry

Serves 4

INGREDIENTS:

**160 gm (5 1/2 oz) ripe
Västerbotten cheese
1 egg yolk, beaten
300 gm (10 oz) puff pastry
dough**
(recipe on page 211)

PREPARATION:

1.
Roll out the puff pastry dough
into 2 1/2 mm (1/10 inch) thickness and cut out 4 rounds,
each 12 cm (4 3/4 inches) in
diameter.

2.
Crumble the cheese and
shape it into four balls. Place
a ball on one half of each
round.

3.
Brush the edges lightly with a
little egg yolk. Fold over the
other half of the dough and
seal the edges, pressing gently
with the fingers.

4.
Brush the puff pastries with
egg yolk and bake them for
about 10 minutes in a 250° C
(500° F) oven.

WERNER:
One should, of course, not
spoil the cheese-maker's work
of art, but in this dish, the
natural taste of the
Västerbotten cheese is
preserved. It is very important
to use fully ripe cheese. It is
when the cheese melts that
the best flavour appears.

I have made experiments with
other cheeses too and found
that for example Kvibille
blue-veined cheese is
excellent. I can imagine that a
fully ripe Grevé would be
suitable too.

An Arctic Symphony of desserts

Cloudberry parfait
Recipe page 168

Blackcurrant mousse
Recipe page 172

Frozen mousse of
arctic raspberries
Queen Silvia
Recipe page 176

Meringue swan
with rhubarb sorbet
Recipe page 180

A symphony of aromatic berries from the wild Scandinavian Arctic pantry.

Sunstroked berries ripened under the warming beams of the Midnight Sun.

Cloudberry from a wet fen. It takes a degree of bravery and a lot of sweat to gather the tasty fruit.

Arctic raspberry with a full round taste. Mmmm . . .! Raspberries with a fresh sharp flavour from a sunbaked slope along the coast.

Lingonberry from a tinder-dry clearing. To be used in an apple pie or as a raw purée to accompany the Swedish "kåldolmar" cabbage rolls.

Blueberries from a shadowy pine forest.

Frost-bitten cranberries and other berries.

In the wilderness pantry you'll find a multitude of berries waiting to be picked. In Sweden everyone can share the bounties provided by nature. This is a freedom. An opportunity. And a large individual responsibility no other nation in Europe provides its citizens.

Pick the berries towards the end of summer or during the first, colourful days of autumn; you probably gazed spellbound at Sven Hörnell's photos on the preceding pages.

Share the forest and mountain fruits. Enjoy nature's garden at the top of the world.

Who knows when you'll next get a fist-full of freshly picked wild strawberries!

"I remember with great pleasure my mother's blueberry mash she offered us children when we were growing up in Switzerland," Werner Vögeli recalls.

"Mashed blueberries with lightly fried pieces of apple bread and whipped cream. And then topped by forest raspberries and wild strawberries.

"Often, of course, we couldn't wait and ate the berries directly after we had picked them. Popped them right in the mouth. Wonderful, and so refreshing. A taste that you never get once the berry has been picked for a while.

"The enormous variety of fresh, wild strawberries to be found growing in the Scandinavian Arctic is a sensation. It can turn any cook crazy with happiness...."

Cloudberries

One short week in June witnesses the annual cloudberry harvest — an uncertain lottery run by nature.

The cloudberry plants are sensitive. Fall easy victim to frost, spring rains, hailstorms and high winds. There are other reasons why the cloudberry harvest can go amiss: perhaps there was a lack of female plants, or maybe the male plants were not up to the task!

Of course, there is the ever important weather. The Scandinavian Arctic can be absolutely glorious with dry, pleasantly warm weather . . . but it can be unkind too. Cold, rainy and windy. Not the kind of weather to encourage insects to fertilise the flowers, which according to the laws of nature they must. But that is nature's way.

The hunt for the elusive cloudberry is intensive. Sometimes aggressive! If the harvest isn't good, the Great Cloudberry War breaks out. Norwegians and Finns rush across into Sweden carrying plastic buckets and juice making machinery. Every berry counts. The cloudberries are picked one berry at a time.

Well . . . most of the tales about people coming to blows and mini juice-making stills being set up are just stories. The only thing that is not exaggerated is the rocketing price of the cloudberry, especially in a bad season. Yet there should be enough cloudberries around for everyone. Someone once estimated that fewer than 4—5 percent of all cloudberries found in the wild are picked.

A devoted picker can gather up to 50 kilos during a day. But the price is a hard one. The picker will have tramped 20—30 kilometers across marshy, moss covered ground. Long arms are needed. And one should expect an aching back. But the "gold" of the moors is a burden worth its price. The taste is stupendous. And very aromatic.

Cloudberries generally grow high in the mountains but can be found in some coast and moor areas.

The period elapsing between the first flowers and the matured fruit is short. Four to six weeks are sufficient if the Midnight Sun has been given the chance to radiate the berries with its generous warmth.

The cloudberries ripen from green to red, and finally end up a rich royal golden yellow. The berries are members of the stone fruit family. In the fruit you'll find small pips, which some like and others spit out.

The cloudberries can be picked semi-ripe and taken home to ripen. But absolutely the best taste comes if you have the patience to wait until the berry has ripened naturally.

"On the continent in Europe few people know of the existence of the cloudberry," says Werner Vögeli. "People call it a variety of different names. It is a shame they are missing such a wonderful fruit. It really is the food of the gods."

The cloudberry can be stored for a long time — and easily. It is best frozen. Sugar isn't needed. Just like raspberries, the cloudberry contains benzo acid — a natural conserving agent.

The cloudberries are delicate tasting berries. They suit just about anything. You decide. Serve them warm or cold. In a parfait, mousse, or ice cream. In a soufflé. On the following pages you'll find some of our favourite recipes.

Cloudberry parfait on hazel-nut pastry with liqueur sauce

Serves 8—10

INGREDIENTS:

8 egg yolks
100 gm (3 1/2 oz) sugar
2 dl (7 fl oz) cloudberry jam, rubbed through a sieve
1 dl (4 fl oz) cloudberry liqueur
6 dl (1 pint) whipping cream

FOR THE NUT PASTRIES:

50 gm (1 1/2 oz) finely ground hazelnuts
50 gm (1 1/2 oz) finely ground almonds
25 gm (slightly less than 1 oz) flour
160 gm (5 1/2 oz) sugar
1 egg
1 egg white
50 gm (1 1/2 oz) melted unsalted butter

FOR THE CLOUDBERRY LIQUEUR SAUCE:

2 egg yolks
40 gm (1 1/2 oz) sugar
1/2 dl (2 fl oz) cloudberry liqueur
2 dl (7 fl oz) whipping cream

PREPARATION OF THE PARFAIT:

1.
Whip the cream — not so hard that it granulates and not too soft — it should be solid and yet smooth.

2.
Beat the egg yolks and sugar to a froth.

3.
Add to the egg froth: cloudberry jam, liqueur and the whipped cream.

4.
Divide the mixture between two cake moulds, about 20 cm (8 inches) in diameter and 3 cm (slightly more than 1 inch) high.

5.
Place the moulds in the freezer for about 3 hours or until the parfait is stiff.

PREPARATION OF THE HAZEL-NUT PASTRIES:

1.
Mix the ground hazelnuts, almonds, flour and sugar.

2.
Beat the whole egg with the egg white. Add the nut mixture and, lastly, the melted butter.

3.
On a sheet of grease-proof paper or on a buttered and floured baking-sheet, form the mixtre into three round cakes, about 20 cm (8 inches) in diameter and 2 mm (1/10 inch) thick.

4.
Bake the nut pastries golden brown in a 200° C (400° F) oven. It takes 8—10 minutes.

PREPARATION OF THE CLOUDBERRY LIQUEUR SAUCE:

1.
Whip the cream into soft peaks.

2.
Beat the egg yolks with the sugar and cloudberry liqueur in a bain-marie or in a saucepan over a very low heat, until the mixture becomes frothy and stiff.

3.
Take the mixture off the heat and continue beating until it is cold.

4.
Finally, fold in the softly whipped cream very gently and the sauce is ready.

5.
Assemble the dessert as shown in the picture.

WERNER:
A great advantage of this dessert is that you can prepare it a few days in advance.

Instead of using cloudberries for this dessert, you can use for example raspberries or currants and the hazelnuts and almonds may be replaced by other kinds of nuts. As cloudberry liqueur may not be available everywhere, you can, of course, replace it by another liqueur or other flavouring.

Nordic grapes

Överkalix in early September. The sun is shining It is like high summer. But we are all wearing long-sleeved clothing. We have to protect ourselves against the mosquitoes . . . You haven't seen mosquitoes until you see those in the Scandinavian Arctic.

We travel to Nybyn, so incredibly beautiful when it swings down towards the Kalix river. We note that the almond potatos are beginning to poke their way up through the soil. On the emptied furrows, filled sacks rest against piles of dug up potato plants.

The earth is black, but soft and embracing.

We walk through some birch thickets. A huge green field with high hedges materializes. Towards one distant edge stands a large forest and moor. Thousands of blackcurrant bushes, the Nordic grapes, standing in long endless straight lines. The clusters are ripe. The silence is broken. A huge, bright red harvesting machine roars into operation. An unnatural sound in the quiet northern environment. A mountain goose heads skywards. Frightened, or perhaps not wanting to get in the way of the harvest.

The machine moves slowly along the line of bushes. Attacking them like a giant ladybird. Great arms reach into the bushes from both sides and vibrate the berries loose. As they fall onto a moving conveyor belt, the stalks and leaves fall leisurely into white boxes. It seems so simple.

The harvesting machine maintains a fast pace. The driver skilfully keeps a straight course. As many berries as possible must be shaken free without being damaged. The bushes must not be harmed either. Two helpers on the giant machine have their hands full keeping up with the pace. There is not a lot of room and the berry boxes are rapidly filled.

We walk along the narrow alleys between the bushes where the machine has already passed. Fantastic. Hardly a berry is left littering the ground and few can be spotted on the bushes.

Osborn Olsson, berry grower from Kungsbacka in the province of Halland, has constructed the machine himself. Together with a Danish grower he has another machine with the same enormous capacity. Further south in Sweden, there are seven or eight smaller, simpler harvesting machines for blackcurrant harvesting.

The blackcurrant was introduced to Europe during the 1600s. But is has only been harvested industrially in the north of Sweden in recent years. Most of the new plantations were built up in the early 1980s.

Just about every village here cultivates the blackcurrant. Carefully, painstakingly and rationally. Many of the larger plantations are to be found about the Pite, Lule, Kalix and Torne river valleys. The largest are around the Kalix river.

Osborn Olsson harvests berries for all the largest growers. He starts in the south and works north as the berries become ready for picking. He has to be in the right place at the right time.

With the help of the hefty machine the harvest, from Piteå in the south to the top of the Torne river valley, can be completed in just 14 days weather permitting.

Sweden's largest berry plantations are sited in the Arctic region. Around 250 hectares have been planted in the last few years.

Almost a third, around 1,000 metric tons annually, of Sweden's berries are grown in the far north. On average the berry bushes provide 4—5 metric tons per hectare. The most profitable bushes can yield up to 6.

Berry bushes rarely yield their best harvest until five or six years of age. In 1988, the Swedish berry growers expect their greatest yields from bushes planted at the beginning of the decade.

Arctic berries are of the highest quality. That is partly due the clean air and water. During the really hot periods when there is little rainfall, the berries are artificially watered.

Sugar content in berries is higher when they can ripen in a climate with long sunny days and light, cool nights. The berries grow strong, survive winter and give good harvests. It is safer to grow berries in the far north of Sweden than in the province of Skåne in the deep south. The biggest problem growing blackcurrants is the threat of frost coming in the fruition stage. And that is not as great a risk in the north because fruiting comes usually when the spring frost is over, in mid-May.

These blackcurrants are also less likely to suffer insect damage than those grown further south. Until now growers have rarely had to resort to the use of chemical insecticides.

"We do get some problems with the berry moth, a little devil that lays eggs towards the end of the summer, jumps from bud to bud before becoming a larva and finally a butterfly," says Karl Gösta Lundmark, berry grower, ex-General, and head of the growers association. "Sadly we have to spray the beasts to rid our plants of them."

What kind of blackcurrant tastes the best?

We tried berries from Korpikylä, Mellalahti, Jänkisjärvi, Öjebyn. We just can't decide, to be honest. All the blackcurrants have a heady aroma under their fiber rich skins. Earlier the blackcurrants were in short supply and very profitable to grow. Today that has changed. There is a surplus. That is why planters, the local authorities and the berry industry as a whole have joined forces to find new profitable opportunities for these "Nordic grapes". New kinds of jams, yoghurts, and other products.

In Överkalix they already make a special juice with an absolutely out-of-this-world taste. If it had been made with white "grapes" it could be sold as an alcohol free alternative to champagne.

For those living a clean, healthy life, the planters are quick to point out that the blackcurrants have three times higher vitamin C levels than oranges, for example. Blackcurrants also boast high levels of B vitamin, iron and potassium.

Senior citizens in the Torne valley tell about the medicinal benefits the blackcurrant provides. Lignite in the berry is supposed to be good against gallstones; tea made from the leaves is marvellous against gout; and the juice is said to work wonders when used to counter coughs and colds. Even heart and circulation problems are helped by the mighty blackcurrant.

There are innumerable local recipes putting the blackcurrant to culinary use. In jams and juices, jellies and mousses, in marmalade or whatever. There is no limit to what can be made using the near miraculous blackcurrant from Sweden's far north. Just try to imagine the enormous opportunities opened up for mouth watering desserts: How about a charlotte, a sorbet or a mousse made from "Nordic grapes"?

Blackcurrant mousse

Serves 4

INGREDIENTS:

2 dl (7 fl oz) whipping cream
20 gm (2/3 oz) sugar
are whipped softly together
1 1/2 dl (6 fl oz) blackcurrant
purée
2 tbls water
50 gm (1 1/2 oz) sugar
are stirred together and
mixed with the cream
3 gelatine leaves (soaked in
water and melted in a bain-
marie) or 1 envelope of
gelatine powder.

PREPARATION:

1.
Add the gelatine to the
mixture and pour it into four
small or one large mould.
Place a slice of sponge-cake
on top. Put the mould(s) in
the refrigerator.

2.
Unmould the mousse and
pour blackcurrant sauce over.
Decorate with a little crème
fraiche.

SAUCE:

1/4 litre (8 fl oz) blackcurrants
1 dl (4 fl oz) sugar
1 dl (4 fl oz) water

1.
Bring sugar and water to the
boil and cool, forming a
syrup.

2.
Liquidize the blackcurrants
and add the syrup until a
coating consistency is
formed.

A Queen among berries

They resemble wild strawberries, look like raspberries, can be confused sometimes with blackberries . . . are red-brown, pale lilac.

"Of all the berries I've eaten or used in recipes, I would say the arctic raspberry is the greatest . . . without a doubt," says an enraptured Werner Vögeli.

"The arctic raspberry has an intensive taste and aroma unmatched by any other berry. It is a taste sensation. I wish everyone in the world could experience the taste . . . It is absolutely heavenly!"

The arctic raspberry is not to be found in large quantities in the far north. It can be found further south but is a rare guest. It is a demanding berry when it comes to being picked too. The good years are few and far between, although when it does grow well there tends to be an abundance. It chooses its home site with care.

Just a few metric tons are picked every year in the Scandinavian Arctic. It demands more work than picking a cloudberry, blueberry or lingonberry and is harder to clean. But patience provides an excellent reward. No other berry, no matter how exclusive or colourful, can give the same rich taste as an arctic raspberry allowed to ripen under the Midnight Sun.

We visit Eva Johansson at Storön outside Kalix. She invites us to try some newly prepared pancakes with an arctic raspberry jam, only lightly sugared, almost natural.

"Heavenly," sighs Werner. "I can understand why Karl von Linné, Sweden's renowned horticulturist, called the arctic raspberry the "Queen of all berries" "

The taste is unusual. An uplifting experience for all who pick the rare berry. The flowers are magnificent. In the midst of summer, in full bloom, they create rolling pastures of deepest pink, like blankets of small roses.

The arctic raspberry can be spotted on mountain slopes, but are most usually found along the coast. They do not like a high oxygen level. You'll mostly find them therefore in areas with a high chalk content soil. You'll also find them in ditches, thickets and scattered around the northern valleys. We have actually spotted arctic raspberries growing along the roadside at several places in the uppermost regions of the Bay of Bothnia. In both Sweden and Finland.

The arctic raspberry clings to the soil with short stringy roots. The plant usually grows to a height varying between 10—30 centimeters.

The berries which don't disappear into the jam jars of those living in the far north, end up in Finland for use in their liquor industry . . . or on plates before diners at the Operakällaren restaurant in Stockholm.

"I once purchased 2 tons of arctic raspberries," recalls Werner. "It was the entire stock available!"

Wild strawberry

Grows in the forest lands, in sunlight glades. Picked in July through September. Can be eaten directly or used to sumptuously decorate a cake, for creams, sauces and ice-cream. A very hardy berry — with a marvellous flavour.

Raspberry

Sun worshipper. Usually found in the southern areas of the Scandinavian Arctic. The further north one travels, the rarer it becomes. Yet the raspberry is a close relative of both the arctic raspberry and the cloudberry.

The raspberry ripens at the end of July or early August. It should be eaten whole and fresh. It also makes a marvellous sauce and freezes well.

Frozen mousse of arctic raspberries "Queen Silvia"

Serves 6

INGREDIENTS:

2 1/2 dl (8 fl oz) purée of arctic raspberries
1 1/4 dl (4 fl oz) whipping cream
2 1/2 dl (8 fl oz) water
150 gm (5 oz) sugar

PREPARATION:

1.
Liquidize or mash and rub through a sieve 400 gm (14 oz) fresh or frozen arctic raspberries. There should be about 2 1/2 dl (8 fl oz) of purée.

2.
Mix the water and sugar in a saucepan. Bring to the boil and cool to a syrup.

3.
Mix in the purée.

4.
Pour the mixture into an electric churn freezer (if available) and churn until almost frozen. Add the unwhipped cream, and continue churning until a smooth and fluffy mousse is formed.

WERNER:
If you do not have an electric ice cream freezer, pour the mixture of purée and syrup into a bowl and place it in the freezer. When it starts setting, take the bowl out and whisk the mixture smooth (preferably with an electric whisk). Repeat the same procedure a couple of times while the mixture is freezing, which takes 3—4 hours. Just before it solidifies completely, add the unwhipped cream, while whisking. Put the bowl back into the freezer. Beat the mousse once more just before serving, in order to make it smooth and fluffy.

SAUCE:

120 gm (4 oz) arctic raspberries
60 gm (2 oz) sugar

Mix the berries and sugar in a saucepan and bring to the boil.
Rub the mixture through a sieve.

HAZELNUT CROWN:

INGREDIENTS:

60 gm (2 oz) sugar
40 gm (1 1/3 oz) ground hazelnuts
20 gm (2/3 oz) flour
2 egg whites

PREPARATION:

On a piece of 1 mm thick carton, draw a star with 6 points, sized approx. 13 cm (5 inches) between the outer points and 8 cm (3 inches) between the inner points. Cut out the star with a sharp knife.

1.
Butter a baking-sheet and sprinkle it lightly with flour.

2.
Mix all ingredients together. Using the pattern, make six stars.

3.
Bake the stars until golden brown in a 200° C (400° F) oven, about 8 minutes.

4.
Leave the baking-sheet to stand in the oven with the door open, preventing the stars from cooling. Remove them, one by one, from the baking-sheet and form them in a glass bowl of suitable size to achieve the desired shape.

CANDY FLOSS
(Recipe on page 213)

A pair of whooping-swans mirror one another in an opening in the newly melted ice. It is spring. Come let us fly together.

Meringue swan
with rhubarb sorbet
in wild raspberry sauce

INGREDIENTS FOR THE
MERINGUE:

**1 dl (4 fl oz) egg whites
160 gm (5 1/2 oz) sugar**

Makes about 7 dl (24 fl oz)
meringue mixture,
10 swans

PREPARATION:

1.
Mix half of the sugar with the
egg white and beat softly.
Add the remaining sugar and
whisk to a stiff foam.

2.
Pipe the meringues in the
shape of swans' wings and
necks onto baking sheets.

3.
Dry in very slow oven
overnight, 50—60°C
(100—125°F).

WILD RASPBERRY SAUCE:
Serves 4:

INGREDIENTS:

**150 gm (5 oz) wild raspberries
1 dl (4 fl oz) syrup of sugar**
(8 cl (3 fl oz) water and
40 gm (1 1/3 oz) sugar are
brought to a boil and cooled)

PREPARATION:

1.
Liquidize or mash the
raspberries and add syrup
until a coating consistency is
formed. Strain through a fine
sieve (this makes about 2 dl
(7 fl oz) sauce).

RHUBARB SORBET:
See recipe on page 182.

FOR THE GARNISH:
**100 gm (3 1/2 oz) wild
strawberries**

PRESENTATION:

Place a ball of rhubarb sorbet
between two meringue wings.
Press a little and fix the neck.
Divide the raspberry sauce
between four plates. Place the
meringue swan in the centre
and sprinkle some wild
strawberries around.

Blackcurrant sorbet

INGREDIENTS:

1/2 litre (18 fl oz) blackcurrant purée
1/2 litre (18 fl oz) water
350 gm (12 oz) sugar
Bring water and sugar to the boil and cool.
For 1/2 litre (18 fl oz) purée you need
about 1 1/4 litres (2 pints)
blackcurrants.

PREPARATION:

1.
Mash the blackcurrants in a mixer or
equivalent and rub through a sieve.

2.
Mix the purée with the syrup of sugar and
put it in an electric churn freezer. Churn until
the sorbet has a smooth consistency.

WERNER:
You may, of course, cook the berries and get
more volume out of them, but I find the sorbet more refreshing, when it is made of raw
berries.
The sorbet may be flavoured with blackcurrant liqueur or aquavit, but, personally, I
prefer the fine flavour of the fresh berries.

Rhubarb sorbet

INGREDIENTS:

300 gm (10 oz) rhubarbs
250 gm (9 oz) sugar
1/2 litre (18 fl oz) water

PREPARATION:

Boil all ingredients together for about 5
minutes, allow to cool and freeze.

Cloudberry sorbet

INGREDIENTS:

1/2 litre (18 fl oz) cloudberry
purée
1/2 litre (18 fl oz) water
350 gm (12 oz) sugar
Bring water and sugar to a boil. Cool.

For 1/2 litre (18 fl oz) purée you need about
1 litre (1 1/2 pints) of cloudberries.

PREPARATION:

Same as for blackcurrant sorbet.

WERNER:
You may flavour the sorbet with cloudberry
liqueur, but I prefer the pure taste of the
berries.

Lingonberry sorbet

INGREDIENTS:
1/2 litre (18 fl oz) lingonberry purée
1/2 litre (18 fl oz) water
350 gm (12 oz) sugar
Bring water and sugar to the boil and cool.
For 1/2 litre (18 fl oz) purée you need about
1 litre (1 3/4 pints) of lingonberries.

PREPARATION:

Same as for blackcurrant sorbet.

Artic raspberry sorbet

Serves 14

INGREDIENTS:

1 kg (2,2 lb) purée of artic raspberries
1 litre (1 1/2 pints) water
600 gm (1 1/3 lb) sugar
Bring water and sugar to the boil. Cool.

For 1 kg (2,2 lb) purée you need about 1,6 kg
(3 1/2 lb) arctic raspberries.

PREPARATION:

Same as for blackcurrant sorbet.

WERNER:
I think the artic raspberries themselves have
such a fantastic aroma and flavour that they
are at their best when prepared as above.
However, you may add for example an egg
white and thus get 1/2 litre (18 fl oz) more in
volume. It makes the sorbet fluffier and more
economical.

You may heighten the flavour with for
example arctic raspberry liqueur or lemon.

Good to know about sorbets:
Frozen berries should be thawed for obtain-
ing the best results. The sorbet may also be
made from fruit-syrups. If you do not pos-
sess an electric churn freezer, put the bowl in
the freezer. When the sorbet starts freezing,
whisk it with an electric whisk, until it
becomes fluffy. Put it back into the freezer
and repeat a few times. Whisk again immediately before serving.

BLACKCURRANT

RHUBARB

CLOUDBERRY

LINGONBERRY

ARCTIC
RASPBERRY

183

Blackcurrant charlotte

Serves 10

INGREDIENTS:

4 egg yolks
40 gm (1 1/3 oz) sugar
whip together until frothy
4 dl (14 fl oz) whipping cream
whip lightly and mix with the
eggs and sugar
1 1/2 dl (6 fl oz) blackcurrant
purée
75 gm (2 1/2 oz) sugar
stir together and put into the
mixture
4 gelatine leaves soaked in
cold water, melted in bain-
marie and mixed with the
other ingredients.

PREPARATION:

1.
Line the moulds, holding
about 2 dl (7 fl oz) with plastic
film. Put slices of Swiss roll,
covering the bottom and the
sides of the bowl, and fill up
with the mixture. Place in the
refrigerator.

2.
Turn out the moulds on
dessert-plates and pour
blackcurrant sauce around the
mousse. Sprinkle with icing
sugar.

SAUCE:

1/4 litre (9 fl oz) blackcurrants
1 dl (4 fl oz) sugar
1 dl (4 fl oz) water

Bring sugar and water to the
boil and cool. Mash the
blackcurrants in a mixer and
add syrup until a coating
consistency is formed.

SWISS ROLL:

3 eggs
1 1/2 dl (6 fl oz) sugar
2 dl (7 fl oz) flour
1 tsp baking powder
2 dl (7 fl oz) blackcurrant jelly
(recipe on page 212)

PREPARATION:

1.
Beat the eggs and sugar.

2.
Mix and sift the flour and
baking powder and stir it into
the egg mixture.

3.
Use a baking-sheet of about
30×40 cm (12×16 inches).
Cover it with greaseproof
paper. Spread the cake
mixture on the paper and
bake it in a 225°C (450°F) oven
for 5—8 minutes.

4.
Turn out the sponge cake on a
greaseproof paper. Spread
blackcurrant jelly on the cake
and roll it up.

Snow eggs
in wild raspberry sauce

Serves 5

INGREDIENTS FOR THE
MERINGUES:

3 egg whites
80 gm (2 2/3 oz) sugar
butter for the moulds

PREPARATION:

1.
Beat the egg whites and sugar
into a firm froth.

2.
Butter the moulds, which
should be round at the
bottom. Fill them with
meringue mixture and bake in
bain-marie for 15—20 minutes
in a 175°C (350°F) oven. Allow
to cool.

INGREDIENTS FOR THE
RASPBERRY SAUCE:

1/2 litre (18 fl oz) raspberries
2 dl (7 fl oz) sugar
2 dl (7 fl oz) water
bring sugar and water to the
boil and cool.

PREPARATION:

Mash the raspberries in a
mixer and add syrup until a
coating consistency is formed.
Sieve.

This batch makes about 7 dl
(24 fl oz) of sauce (so, it may
be reduced).

Pour a little more than 1/2 dl
(2 fl oz) of sauce on each plate
and place meringue balls on
the sauce.

WERNER:
You may use any type of fresh
berries in a similar way.

The sweetness of the berries
differs and, therefore, you
must decide yourself how
much sugar syrup to use.

The classic way of baking
meringues is poaching them
in vanilla flavoured milk on
the stove, but baking them in
the oven is easier.

Frozen soufflé of arctic raspberries

Serves 6

INGREDIENTS:

250 gm (8 1/2 oz) purée of arctic raspberries
3 egg yolks
1 1/2 dl (6 fl oz) whipping cream
200 gm (7 oz) sugar
1/2 dl (2 fl oz) water
6 soufflé moulds

PREPARATION:

1.
Mix water and sugar in a saucepan and boil for a few minutes. An old reliable method to see whether the syrup is ready is the following. Loop a thin wire. Dip it in the syrup and blow carefully (just like blowing soap-bubbles). The syrup should stay in the loop.

2.
Beat the egg yolks in a bowl. Add the warm syrup, whisking continuously until the mixture is cold, white and frothy.

3.
Add the purée and beat the mixture frothy again.

4.
Whip the cream and stir in carefully.

MACAROONS
(almond pastries)
Makes 6

50 gm (1 1/2 oz) almond paste
2 tsp sugar
2 tsp egg white
2 tbls arctic raspberry liqueur

PREPARATION:

1.
Make a dough of all the ingredients (except the liqueur).

2.
Form it into a 1 cm (approx 1/2 inch) thick roll.

3.
Cut the roll into 1 1/2 cm (3/5 inch) long pieces.

4.
Cover a baking-sheet with greaseproof paper. Put the pieces of dough on the paper and flatten them out to 1/2 cm (1/5 inch) height.

5.
Bake them golden brown at 200°C (400°F) for about 8 minutes. Allow to cool and steep in the liqueur.

6.
Tie bands of double thickness greaseproof paper around the outside of the soufflé dishes to stand 3—4 cm (1 1/2 inch) above the rims. Butter the joining edges of the paper so that they stick together. Half-fill each dish with the mousse, place a macaroon on top and then fill up with the remaining mousse so that it reaches slightly over the top of the edge of the dish.

7.
Refrigerate the soufflés.

8.
Remove from the refrigerator 1/2 hour before serving so that the soufflés are soft and creamy.

Cloudberry soufflé with liqueur-flavoured cream

Serves 4—5

INGREDIENTS:

2 1/2 dl (8 fl oz) milk
2 tbls flour
4 egg yolks
3 tbls sugar
50 gm (1 2/3 oz) fresh or frozen and thawed cloudberries
50 gm (1 2/3) cloudberry jam
5 egg whites
1 tbls butter and
1 tbls sugar (for the mould)

Use a soufflé dish, 18 cm (7 inches) in diameter and 6 cm (2 1/2 inches) high — enough for 4—5 portions.

PREPARATION OF THE SOUFFLE:

1.
Put the flour in a saucepan (not aluminium). Pour the milk over, whisking continuously to avoid lumps. Add egg yolks and sugar.

2.
Bring the mixture to the boil, while whisking. Take it off the heat and allow to cool a little.

3.
Meanwhile, beat the egg whites until stiff.

4.
Mix the cloudberry jam and the fresh berries with the milk and egg yolk mixture and, last, gently fold in the egg whites.

5.
Pour the soufflé mixture into the buttered and sugared soufflé dish.

6.
Bake in a 200°C (400°F) oven for 20—25 minutes. Cover with grease-proof paper at the end if the surface starts to get too brown.

7.
Sprinkle the soufflé with icing sugar and serve immediately with the liqueur-flavoured cream.

LIQUEUR-FLAVOURED CREAM:

INGREDIENTS:

1 1/2 dl (6 fl oz) whipping cream
1 tbls sugar
1 tbls cloudberry liqueur

PREPARATION:

Whip the cream with half of the sugar and pour it into a dish. Sprinkle the remaining sugar over and add the liqueur.

WERNER:
It is very important that the mould is well buttered up

to the edge. The sugar should be sprinkled all over.
If you add a pinch of salt to the egg whites, they will rise more easily.

Midnight Sun over Kebnekaise

Kebnekaise is Sweden's highest mountain, 2,111 metres above sea level. Kebnekaise was first climbed in 1883 by Frenchman Charles Rabot.

Today tourists acquainted with climbing, and in good condition, can reach the top in a day with even limited mountaineering experience. Professional mountaineers act as guides.

At 1,880 metres you will find Sweden's highest building. The Kebnekaise mountain chalet. It provides a resting point before the final charge through the snow and to the summit to be greeted with a magnificent view.

From the north and south peaks one can see over 100 kilometres into the vast Sarek national park, Europe's second largest. Padjelanta, west of Sarek, is Europe's last untouched wilderness, almost 2,000 square kilometres! A panoramic view of the Kebnekaise range. Snow lies deep and crisp all year round.

Large powerful mountain peaks point resolutely heavenwards: Knivkammen, Drakryggen, Kaskatjåkka, and the largest of them all, Kebnekaise. The photograph has been taken under the Midnight Sun — in May.

The Midnight Sun is a natural phenomenon north of the arctic circle from mid-May until early August. It is just one long day, when the night light gradually shifts to a shimmering red. The sun never sets below the horizon.

"I wake every morning without a new day having started," says mountain photographer Sven Hörnell who took these.

196

Oven-baked ice-cream Kebnekaise

INGREDIENTS:

150 gm (5 oz) almond pastry
(recipe on page 213)
3 tbls cloudberry jam
6 dl (1 pint) vanilla ice-cream
(recipe on page 213)
4 egg whites
1 dl (4 fl oz) sugar
(+ a little to sprinkle over)

PREPARATION:

1.
Place the almond pastry on a round plate and spread the cloudberry jam on it.

2.
Spread the ice-cream over it and place the plate in the freezer.

3.
Meanwhile, whip the egg whites and sugar to a stiff foam.

4.
Take the plate out of the freezer and spread the egg white evenly over the ice-cream.

5.
Sprinkle a little sugar all over and bake it golden brown in the oven at 250°C (500°F) for about 5 minutes.

CLOUDBERRY SAUCE:

2 dl (7 fl oz) fresh or frozen and thawed cloudberries, rubbed through a sieve
2 tbls sugar
1 dl (4 fl oz) water

PREPARATION:

1.
First, make the syrup (bring sugar and water to the boil and allow to cool).

2.
Rub the cloudberries through a sieve and stir them with the syrup.

WERNER:
Instead of almond pastry, you may use an ordinary sponge cake.

This dessert can be prepared in advance (however not as early as the day before) and then put into the oven before serving.

Iced parfait from the Land of the Midnight Sun

Serves 10

Two moulds with detachable bottoms, about 20 cm (8 inches) in diameter. Take the bottoms away, as you do not need them.

INGREDIENTS FOR THE PARFAIT:

8 egg yolks
100 gm (3 1/2 oz) sugar
1 dl (4 fl oz) cloudberry jam, (rubbed through a sieve)
3 tbls cloudberry liqueur
1 dl (4 fl oz) arctic raspberry jam (rubbed through a sieve)
3 tbls arctic cloudberry liqueur
a few drops of lemon
6 dl (1 pint) whipping cream

FOR DECORATING THE CAKE:

1 dl (4 fl oz) arctic raspberry jam
1 dl (4 fl oz) cloudberry jam (both rubbed through a sieve)

PREPARATION:

1.
Beat the egg yolks and sugar until frothy. Divide the mixture between two bowls.

2.
Whip the cream.

3.
To one of the bowls, add the cloudberry jam, cloudberry liqueur and 2—3 drops of lemon. Stir in half of the whipped cream.

4.
To the other bowl, add the arctic raspberry jam and liqueur, 2—3 drops of lemon and the remaining cream.

5.
Take a cake carton or two pieces of cardboard and cover them with greaseproof paper. Place the moulds (without bottom) on the sheets and fill them with the parfait mixture, one flavour in each.

6.
Place them in the freezer for about 3 hours or until the parfait is stiff.

FOR THE HAZELNUT PASTRY ROUNDS:

100 gm (3 1/2 oz) finely ground hazelnuts
1 egg
1 egg white
25 gm (1 oz) flour
160 gm (5 1/2 oz) sugar
50 gm (1 3/4 oz) melted, unsalted butter

PREPARATION:

Mix all ingredients. On greaseproof paper, spread the mixture into three rounds, about 20 cm (8 inches) in diameter and 2 mm (1/10

inch) thick. Bake them golden brown in a 200°C (400 °F) oven, 5—6 minutes.

ASSEMBLING THE DESSERT:

Place a hazelnut round on a plate, then one parfait on it. Continue with the second round, the other parfait and finish with the third hazelnut round.

On top of everything, spread
1 dl (4 fl oz) arctic raspberry
jam and, in the center of it, 1
dl (4 fl oz) cloudberry jam,
which is drawn out with the
point of a knife like rays of
sunshine.

The lingonberry is vacuumed clean at the plant of wholesaler Norrfrys in Haparanda. Tons of berries from all over northern Scandinavia are cleaned at the plant.

In Finland several alcoholic beverages are made using the berries from the Scandinavian Arctic. In Pyhäjoki they make a cloudberry liqueur known as Red Icebreaker.

The red gold of the forest

Lingonberry is the most common of all the wild berries found in the Scandinavian Arctic. The forests' 'red gold' found in plentiful quantities. Ripen in September. It is not unusual to be able to pick berries through to late October. The lingonberries grow in the forests and on mountain slopes, usually in dry thickets. Amongst moss and lichen. Where the reindeer wander.

Lingonberries are hardy fruit. Need little sugar to preserve. Like cloudberries, they contain benzoic acid. It is impossible to estimate how many tons are picked every year; nor how many jam jars are filled.

The lingonberry has always comprised an essential ingredient in most northern households. Used with milk and thin bread, with meat, and fish — yes, the Norwegians eat lingonberry with cod.

"I cannot imagine anything nicer than lingonberry to accompany everyday Swedish food," comments Werner Vögeli. "Raw crushed lingonberries with meatballs, bacon pancakes and cabbage rolls is a total delicacy."

Sweden is one of the world's largest lingonberry producing nations. The red gold of the forest grows everywhere. Many pick lingonberry to raise some extra cash. Much is exported.

Blueberry

Blueberry, also known as bilberry or whortleberry, loves sheltering in the cooling shadows of the forest. As the forest lands are cut back, we find fewer blueberries.

Correct.

But there is no danger of that happening in the Scandinavian Arctic yet. There are more than enough blueberries to go around. Fact is, we utilise just five percent of the blueberries that are available.

The small, round berries, covered with a waxlike skin to keep the humidity deep inside the berry, ripen earlier than lingonberries One can find them in early August if the weather has been kind.

Every year the blueberry drops its leaves. They die at the onset of Autumn. Around the actual stalk the blueberry plant has a wreath with multi-coloured leaves: red, brown, green and shiny black.

The wild blueberry should not be confused with the cultivated American giant blueberry which is often sold as a bush for planting in gardens. As we said earlier, no cultivated plant can provide the same taste sensations as those that have grown in the wild.

Blueberries are extremely suitable for all jams, juices for desserts and cakes.

Crowberry

The mountain crowberry rather resembles the ordinary blueberry but has a milder, somehow fresher taste. However, it lacks character. The berry is darker than the blueberry, somewhat smaller.

In Finland more crowberries are picked than in Sweden. We discovered this after having spoken to people during our journey. At the Vita Renen Restaurant at the Hotel Pohjanhovi in Rovaniemi we found a remarkable parfait made with crowberries.

In northern Norway, the locals use a mousse of crowberries together with fish liver. Some Swedish Laplanders eat freshly picked crowberries with their reindeer milk.

Around five kilos of wild berries per person are picked annually in the Nordic region. For trade and industry a normal year can be broken down in the following fashion.

	From the Nordic Area	From the Arctic Region
Blueberry	10 million kilos	2 million kilos
Lingon-berry	20 million kilos	4 million kilos
Cloud-berry	1.5 million kilos	600—800,000 kilos
Wild Rasp-berry	10,000 kilos	2,000 kilos
Cran-berry	200,000—300,000 (mainly Finland)	

Probably as many more berries are picked, but remain in the homes of those who picked them. Around 40 million kilos of wild berries are picked in Sweden alone every year.

"That represents just 4—5 percent of everything that could be picked," says Alan Lehto, professional berry buyer at Haparanda. "In Sweden alone we estimate that the number of pickable wild berries must be in the region of 320,000 metric tons; 200,000 tons of blueberry and 120,000 tons of lingonberry"

Operakällaren's apple cake

Serves 4

INGREDIENTS:

4 middle-sized, sourish apples,
preferably Signe Tillisch
3 dl (1/2 pint) lingonberries, fresh or frozen
1 dl (4 fl oz) sugar
Mix sugar and lingonberries and mash them lightly
Makes about 2 dl ((7 fl oz)

ALMOND PASTE:

100 gm (3 1/2 oz) butter
100 gm (3 1/2 oz) genuine almond paste
2 eggs
2 tbls flour

PREPARATION:

1.
Start with the almond paste.

2.
Stir the butter and almond paste until white and fluffy.

3.
Stir in the eggs, one by one, and the flour.

4.
Peel and core the apples.

5.
Butter and flour either four small moulds, about 10 cm (4 inches) in diameter and 4 1/2 cm (2 inches) high, or one large mould.

6.
Divide the mixture between the four moulds or put all of it in the large one. Place the apples in it and fill the holes with the mashed lingonberries.

7.
Bake in a 180°C (350°F) oven for about 30 minutes.

Bring the leftover lingonberries to the boil and fill the holes of the apples once more after baking, the first will sink a little.

Serve whipped cream with the cake.

204

Individual blueberry pies with whipped cream

Serves 4

INGREDIENTS:

5 dl (17 fl oz) blueberries
4 tbls sugar
1 tsp corn-flour

FOR THE PASTRY DOUGH:

100 gm (3 1/2 oz) butter
100 gm (3 1/2 oz) sugar
1 egg
1/4 dl (1 fl oz) milk
200 gm (7 oz) flour

PREPARATION:

1.
Mix the butter, sugar, egg and milk.

2.
Add the flour without working the dough too much, as it will become tough.

3.
Let the dough rest in the refrigerator for 30 minutes.

4.
Divide the blueberries between four individual moulds. Mix the sugar with the corn flour and sprinkle over the berries.

5.
Roll out the dough to about 3 mm (1/10 inch) thickness and cut out a lid for each mould. Cover and neaten the edges. The easiest way of getting the correct size of the lids is to use a mould upside down as a pattern, (of course before you put the blueberries in).

6.
Brush with beaten egg and sprinkle with sugar.

7.
Bake in a 200° C (400° F) oven for about 15 minutes.

Serve the pies warm (but not too hot) with whipped cream.

WERNER:
Pastry dough left over may be wrapped up well and kept in the refrigerator for a couple of days. You can also freeze it.

Mother Ida's blueberry mash

Mashed blueberries, mixed with sugar, and croûtons, fried in butter, served lukewarm with whipped cream.

Garnish, if you wish, with a few wild raspberries or wild strawberries.

Some good recipes for basics

Feathered game stock

INGREDIENTS:
1 kg (2,2 lb) carcasses of game birds
400 gm (14 oz) mirepoix
2 tbls cooking oil
2 litres (3 pints) water

PREPARATION:
1.
Cut the carcasses in pieces and brown them in the oil in a suitable pan. After they have begun to colour add the mirepoix, stir thoroughly, and allow to brown for a little longer.
2.
Add the water, with a wooden spoon scrape the caramelised debris from the bottom of the pan and bring to the boil.
3.
Let the stock simmer for 2 hours, skimming from time to time.
4.
Strain the stock and reduce it until about 1/2 litre (17 fl oz) remains.

WERNER:
This is a neutral stock. If it is further reduced until only 2 cl (2/3 fl oz) remain, it becomes a game extract.

The stock can be enriched, depending on its eventual use.
The bones can be deglazed with cognac, for example, and 1/2 litre (17 fl oz) of the water replaced with 1/2 bottle of red wine.

The stock can be thickened by sprinkling a tablespoon of flour over the bones in the latter stages of browning, or by adding a table spoon of corn-flour, which has been dissolved in a little water or wine. All depends on the intended use of the stock.

Ordinary game stock:
Replace the game bird carcasses with bones from any other kind of game.

Basic mirepoix

INGREDIENTS:

onions
carrots
celery
parsley stalks

PREPARATION:
Peel the onions and the carrots. Cut up equal quantities of onion, carrot and celery into 1 cm cubes.

The above ingredients can be replaced by other vegetables and herbs, for example garlic, shallots, mushroom stalks and trimmings, leeks, thyme, bay leaf etc

Fish sauce

INGREDIENTS:

1 litre (1 1/2 pints) fish stock
45 gm (1 1/2 oz) butter
90 gm (3 oz) butter to finish the sauce
4 tbls flour
1 1/2 dl (6 fl oz) dry white wine
1 dl (4 fl oz) whipping cream
salt and freshly ground white pepper
lemon juice

PREPARATION:
1.
Melt the butter in a saucepan and stir in the flour. Let this roux cook over a low heat for a couple of minutes without colouring, stirring from time to time.
2.
Add the fish stock, whisking constantly. Allow to simmer for 45 minutes, stirring occasionally.
3.
Remove the pan from the heat. There should be about 5 dl (17 fl oz) of sauce left.
4.
Add the white wine, cream and remainder of butter. Whisk for about 5 minutes with an electric whisk. Manual whisking does not give the same volume or smoothness to the sauce as an electric whisk.

WERNER:
This sauce is ideal for preparing in advance. It can be reheated without loss of quality and will not separate.
The taste can be further improved by the addition of the reduced cooking liquid from the fish in question.
The sauce can, of course, be named after the type of wine which is used, for example Chablis sauce, Riesling sauce, or be simply called white wine sauce.

FISH STOCK: see page 60
Salmon bones can be replaced by other fish bones, preferably those from flat fish, for example turbot.

Chicken stock

INGREDIENTS:

1 boiling fowl, eviscerated and cut into 8 pieces
the giblets
1 bouquet garni
5 white peppercorns
2 cloves
1 large onion, peeled, sliced in two through the root
and browned in a hot dry frying-pan
salt

PREPARATION:
1.
Rince the pieces of the bird well and place them in a suitable pot with the giblets. Cover them with cold water and bring to the boil.
2.
Allow to simmer for 5 minutes and skim. Add the salt, spices and vegetables and simmer until the chicken is cooked, skimming from time to time. Strain.

WERNER:
To improve the flavour one can add the white of a leek, a piece of celery or celeriac and a few small carrots. Remove these vegetables as soon as they are cooked and serve them separately with vinaigrette or simply as they are. Of course one must not add too many vegetables and take away the taste of the chicken.
The chicken itself can be used for salads, vol au vents, croquettes, forcemeat etc.
The stock can be frozen for later use.

Bouquet garni

INGREDIENTS:

the green of a leek
at least 3 parsley stalks
1 sprig of thyme
1 bay leaf

PREPARATION:
Tie the ingredients together on one end of a piece of string.
Tie the other end to the handle of the pot — this makes it easier to find and remove the bouquet later.

Butter sauce (beurre blanc)

Serves 4

INGREDIENTS:

1 dl (4 fl oz) white wine
1/2 dl (2 fl oz) whipping cream
1 dl (4 fl oz) vinegar (preferably white
wine vinegar)
2—3 shallots, finely chopped
200 gm (14 oz) butter, softened
lemon juice
salt and freshly ground white pepper

PREPARATION:
1.
Place the shallots and vinegar in a small
thick-bottomed saucepan and reduce until
the vinegar has almost completely evaporated. The shallots should not be dry, but
moist and sticky.
2.
Add the cream and bring to the boil.
3.
Add the softened butter piece by piece,
whisking continuously, over a low heat.
4.
Finish with a few drops of lemon juice,
salt and freshly ground white pepper.
5.
For an absolutely smooth sauce, pass
through a strainer to remove the shallot,
but this is not at all necessary.

BEURRE ROUGE
The recipe and preparation is as above,
but the white wine and white wine vinegar are replaced by red wine and red wine
vinegar and the cream is omitted.

WERNER:
I have seen, prepared and eaten many
varieties of beurre blanc used in different
ways in different dishes, with a reduction
of vinegar, white wine, a specific kind of
white wine, with cream, without cream.
But one thing is very important — use
fresh butter, that is to say a newly opened
packet which has not been tainted by any
smell from the refrigerator.

The uses of beurre blanc are many: first
and most importantly with fish and shell-
fish dishes, but also with vegetables, for
example asparagus, artichoke hearts,
beetroot, leeks, and so on.

If one uses a specific kind of wine, one
can name the butter sauce after it.

Potatoes for croquettes

INGREDIENTS:

400 gm (17 oz) peeled potatoes
2 egg yolks
a pinch of salt
grated nutmeg

PREPARATION:
1.
Cook the potatoes in salted water, which
is then discarded.
2.
Put the pan in a 200°C (400°F) oven for 5
minutes to dry the potatoes (or let stand
uncovered over a low heat).
3.
Mash the potatoes and add the egg yolks
and a little grated nutmeg.

The potatoes can be formed into different
shapes:

Pommes William — pear-shaped

Croquettes — cork-shaped

Croquettes can be coated in ground
almonds instead of breadcrumbs, for
variety.

POMMES WILLIAM
1.
Pipe the mashed potatoes through a
nozzle onto a plate, shaping them like
pears. Refrigerate to make them firm.
2.
Dip in lightly whisked egg white and
cover them with homemade breadcrumbs
mixed with flaked almonds.
3.
Deep-fry them in hot oil until golden
brown.

POTATO CROQUETTES
1.
Pipe the mashed potatoes through a thick
nozzle onto greaseproof paper and cut into cork sized lengths. Refrigerate.
2.
Dip the croquettes in lightly whisked egg
white and cover them with homemade
breadcrumbs, ensuring that there are no
gaps.
3.
Deep-fry them in hot oil until golden
brown.

Puff pastry

INGREDIENTS:

500 gm (1,1 lbs) flour
100 gm (3 1/2 oz) butter at room tempera-
ture
2 1/2 dl (8 fl oz) iced water
approx 10 gm (1/3 oz) salt

FOR USE IN THE ROLLING:
500 gm (1,1 lb) butter
flour

The recipe makes 1,3 kg (3 lb) of puff
pastry.

PREPARATION:
1.
Mix together the flour, salt and the 100
gm (3 1/2 oz) butter at room temperature.
2.
Add the iced water little by little until a
smooth elastic dough is formed. Wrap it
in a damp towel and refrigerate for about
a 1/2 hour.
3.
Roll out the dough into a rectangle 50 cm
(20 inches) long, 35 cm (14 inches) wide
and 4 mm (1/6 inch) thick. Remove as
much of the loose flour as possible.
4.
Flatten out the butter so that it covers half
of the pastry, leaving a 1 cm (approx 1/2
inch) butter-free border. Fold the other
half of the pastry over the butter, press
the edges together and tuck in the corners
so that the butter is completely enclosed.
5.
Roll out this packet into a rectangle of
40—45 cm (16—18 inches) long and 20 cm
(8 inches) wide, and fold it into three.
Turn the packet through 90 degrees and
roll it out into a rectangle 50—60 cm
(20—24 inches) long but the same width.
Fold in the two edges to the middle and
fold again, i.e. fold it into four. All the
loose flour should be removed. Wrap the
pastry in a damp towel, or better still in
greaseproof paper inside a damp towel,
and refrigerate for about 3 hours.

When the pastry is removed from the
refrigerator, step 5 must be repeated.
Then the pastry is ready to use at once or
freeze.

WERNER:
In the refrigerator the puff pastry can be
kept tightly wrapped in cellophane or in a
plastic bag for a maximum of one week.
In the freezer, if it is well wrapped in a
freeze bag and kitchen foil, it will keep for
a maximum of one month. Homemade
puff pastry can lose its elasticity if it is
stored wrongly or for too long.
PUFF PASTRY BOUCHEES — see also
page 60.

Uncooked lingonberry preserve

INGREDIENTS:

1 litre (1 1/2 pints) lingonberries
2 dl (7 fl oz) fine powdered white sugar

PREPARATION:
1.
Clean and rinse the berries.
2.
Crush them lightly in a bowl.
3.
Add the sugar and stir until it has dissolved.

WERNER:
This preserve is one of my absolute favourites and can be used in many ways: with home cooking such as potato pancakes, bacon pancakes, "kroppkakor" — a kind of dumpling filled with ground pork, stuffed cabbage rolls and so on.

The preserve can also be warmed and served with furred game dishes such as reindeer, elk, venison and hare as well as with all dishes made with feathered game.

Blackcurrant jelly

INGREDIENTS:

1 litre (1 1/2 pints) blackcurrants
2 dl (7 fl oz) water
9 dl (32 fl oz) powdered white sugar per litre of juice

PREPARATION:
1.
Clean and rinse the berries, leaving the stalks on.
2.
Bring the water to the boil and cook the berries in it for about 10 minutes. Press the berries against the side of the pot from time to time so that they release their juice.
3.
Strain the juice, allowing it to drain well.
4.
Measure the amount of juice.
5.
Boil it and add the requisite amount of sugar a little at a time. Simmer for 10—15 minutes.
6.
Test by dipping a teaspoon into the mixture. If it sticks, the jelly is ready.

7.
Skim and pour into warm clean dry jars.

WERNER:
Do not use berries which are too ripe. There is more pectin in berries which are under-ripe and the jelly sets and tastes better.

If one uses frozen berries, their volume decreases after rinsing, so measure then, not before, otherwise all the amounts will be wrong.

Rowanberry jelly

INGREDIENTS:

1 litre (1 1/2 pints) rowanberries, frost-bitten
200 gm (7 oz) cooking apples
3 dl (10 fl oz) water
9 dl (32 fl oz) powdered white sugar per litre of juice

PREPARATION:
1.
Clean and rinse the berries. Remove stalk and core the apple. Cut the apple in half and slice it thinly.
2.
Boil the water and cook the apple slices and berries in it for 10 minutes. Press the fruit against the side of the pot from time to time so that they release their juices.
3.
Strain and allow to drain well.
4.
Measure the amount of juice.
5.
Boil it and add the requisite amount of sugar little by little. Simmer for 10—15 minutes.
6.
Test by dipping a teaspoon into the mixture. If it sticks, the jelly is ready.
7.
Skim and pour into warm clean dry jars.

WERNER:
Possessing a freezer is a great advantage, as one can then pick the berries when they are just ripe. But one has to freeze them before preparing. If one waits for the first frost to come, the quality of the berries may deteriorate.

Cloudberry jam

INGREDIENTS:

1 kg (2,2 lb) fresh cloudberries
900 gm (2 lb) powdered white sugar

PREPARATION:

1.
Clean the berries, rinse them and mix them with the sugar.

2.
Place them in a pan, bring slowly to the boil and simmer for 15 minutes.

3.
Skim. As soon as the berries have sunk into the mixture and are evenly dispersed, the preserve is ready.

4.
Immediately pour the jam into screw-topped glass jars.

WERNER:
Because most households nowadays have a freezer, it is better to make a small amount at a time, for example 1 kg (2,2 lb) as described above. Then it is not necessary to add any preservative — the jam will keep in the refrigerator for 3—4 weeks without developing mould. The fresh berries you have over can be frozen.

An advantage of freezing the berries is that they can be used for many things apart from jam, for example in sauces, mousses, puddings, pies, warmed with a little sugar with vanilla ice-cream, for garnishes and so on.

It is advisable to freeze the berries in smaller amounts, making it easy to thaw a little when required.

Use a roomy pan for making this jam because it boils over easily.

Vanilla ice-cream

Approx 1 1/2 litres (2 1/4 pints) ice-cream

INGREDIENTS:

1 litre (1 1/2 pints) thin cream
200 gm (7 oz) white powdered sugar
10 egg yolks
1 vanilla pod

PREPARATION:

1.
Split the vanilla pod into two lengthways and scrape out all of the inside carefully. To ensure that the vanilla will not form lumps in the cream, it can be well mixed at this stage with a spoonful of the sugar.

2.
Place the thin cream, the vanilla pod and its contents into a saucepan and bring to the boil.

3.
Meanwhile, whisk the egg yolks and the sugar together until the yolks become pale.

4.
After removing the vanilla pod, pour the hot cream over the eggs and sugar, whisking vigorously.

5.
Pour the mixture back into the saucepan and over a low heat let the mixture thicken to a coating consistency.

6.
Place the bottom of the pan in a bowl of iced water and whisk the mixture until it is cool.

7.
Freeze in an ice-cream maker.

Spun sugar

200 gm (7 oz) sugar
1 dl (4 fl oz) water

Boil the sugar and the water until the sugar just begins to change colour, not an instant longer. The temperature at this stage is about 155—160°C (310°F). Put the pan on ice for a few seconds so that the cooking is halted. The next stage must begin immediately and the best utensil to use for this is a balloon whisk which has been sawn in half creating a cirkle of metal spikes. Dip the spikes into the sugar and flick the sugar onto a sheet of grease-proof paper or foil.

The resulting strands can be shaped as required: for example into small nests, topped with a hazel-nut crown filled with frozen mousse and a sauce as in the recipe for Frozen arctic raspberry mousse Queen Silvia on page 176.

Almond pastry case

INGREDIENTS:

100 gm (3 1/2 oz) ground almond paste
50 gm (1 3/4 oz) unsalted butter
2 eggs
1 tbls flour

PREPARATION:

1.
Whisk the almond paste with the butter until it turns white.

2.
Stir in the eggs, one at a time, and then the flour.

3.
Bake in a 180°C (350°F) oven in a baking tin or flan ring for about 35 minutes.

Index

Salmon mousseline in puff pastry "Queen Silvia". Page 62.

Place lean, well-trimmed, minced beef on a slice of rye or wholewheat bread. Arrange a circle of bleak roe caviar on top and gently slip an egg yolk into the centre. Sprinkle with finely chopped chives. Serve with capers and chopped oinon.

Mousse of snowgrouse served cold. Page 114.

Operakällaren's apple cake. Page 204.

Desserts

Some additional recipes

A few are accompaniments to previous dishes; some are perfect on their own or can be combined with other dishes from the larder of the Scandinavian Arctic.

SAUCES, DRESSINGS

FOR GAME

FOR FISH

FOR DESSERTS

Some good recipes for basics

Operakällaren's apple cake. Page 204

PHOTOGRAPHS

Gunnar Bergbom
4, 54, 56, 166, 167, 174, 175, 202, 203, 212

Sven Hörnell
Cover (large photograph), 52, 96, 162, 192, 194, 196

Frank A Jenssen
74

Lasse Johansson
55

Per Kagrell
4, 12, 13, 14, 66, 67, 68, 69, 106, 107, 120, 121, 122, 123, 124, 125, 126, 127, 128, 132, 133, 178, 179

Hans Köster
57

Tony Landberg
8, 9, 10, 11, 129, 202

Björn Lindberg
16, 18, 20, 22, 24, 26, 28, 30, 32, 34, 36, 38, 40, 42, 44, 46, 48, 50, 58, 60, 63, 64, 70, 82, 84, 86, 88, 90, 92, 94, 102, 104, 108, 110, 112, 114, 116, 134, 136, 138, 140, 142, 144, 146, 148, 156, 160, 164, 168, 172, 176, 180, 182, 184, 186, 188, 190, 198, 200, 204, 206, 208, 213, 214, 215, 216

Kalle Melander
Cover (small photographs)

Tommy Pedersen
4, 72, 76, 77, 78, 79, 81, 158, 159, 170, 171, 202, 203

Bertil Pettersson/N
98, 99, 100, 101, 118, 150, 152, 153, 154, 166

THANK YOU!
We would like to thank everyone who has helped us with this book. And a very special thanks to Karin Dahlgren and Ove Eriksson.